"Great stuff, well-organized and easy to read! I like the idea and the writing a lot."
Richard Tavener, Nationally Syndicated Radio Show and Webcast Host,
Author of *Just Say YES!, 365 Ideas On How To Start, Grow & Enjoy Your Own Business*

"Many home business owners waste precious time and money buying and using the wrong software programs -- while underutilizing the capabilities of their existing software. Joshua's tips will help home business owners make the most of their computing tools and get the best deals on PC-related purchases -- without the need to always depend on an expensive tech consultant."
Paul and Sarah Edwards, Authors of 14 books including *Working from Home*

"I would hope that most reputable tech consultants would handle their clients in such a manner that this book wouldn't be necessary. But I know that's dreaming. Joshua's book is full of solid best practices. I even learned a few tips myself. Joshua's tips will help small businesses save both money and data."
Larry Lentz, MCSE + Internet, MCDBA, GoldMine Certified Professional,
Lentz Computer Services, San Antonio

"I know firsthand how important it is to maximize office technology, while minimizing costs. At the risk of alienating my own tech consultant, I look forward to using this book."
James K. Roosa, Esq., Small Business Lawyer, Cleveland

"Computer-related books usually don't hold my interest, but Joshua's did. It's well organized, written in layperson terms and right to the point."
Gregg Bernicker, CPA, Gregg Bernicker & Associates, P.C., Hazlet, New Jersey

"... a must read for anyone who has to worry about what happens after an employee pushes the power-on button on a PC."
Andy Walker, Technology Writer, Cyberwalker Media Syndicate, Toronto

"Joshua's book is exactly what small business owners need as a reference tool and toolbox – in our own jargon."
Marty Fletcher, Controller, Chefs International, Point Pleasant Beach, New Jersey

"I used to be amazed at how businesses had done so little to maximize their employee productivity and tech investments. Everyone is just too 'busy' to figure out a better way. Now they won't have an excuse. Joshua's book is a checklist to increase your tech efficiency!"
Peggy Duncan, Efficiency Consultant, Author of *Put Time Management to Work: Get Organized, Streamline Processes, Use the Right Technology*

"Finally, I've found a book that helps me quickly decide whether to invest my time and in-house resources on a technology challenge, or pick up the phone and outsource -- and pay fees that, in hindsight, may have been unnecessary."
Tom Tshontikidis, CFO, Ivy Sea, San Francisco

"Joshua helps small businesses plan, implement and protect computer systems -- how to save money, not only in the short term, but also down the road by avoiding pitfalls. I wish I had had this book when I was implementing our computer systems."
Charles Fisher, Internal Guru, Charles L. Youngman Engineering, Salem, Oregon

"... worth the price of admission, particularly for those of us nontechnical folks."
Monnie Ryan, Managing Editor, *The Business Journal*, Youngstown, Ohio

"The 80/20 Principle teaches us that eighty percent of what we do is routine and twenty percent is critical. Computer consultants should buy a copy of this book for every one of their clients and use the book as a tool for teaching how to do the routine eighty percent."
Wayne Messick, COO, *Family Busi~~~ ~~*

"*Finally, a good reference focusing on the client without jargon or talking down to anyone! It hits the highlights and gives enough information to ask informed questions and make intelligent decisions. This book will make my clients happier and my job easier!*"
> Sid Plait, Senior Computer Consultant, Plait Solutions, Atlanta

"*Joshua's book is a great reference for immediate concerns – and excellent for cover-to-cover reading when time allows.*"
> Katherine Caughran, CPP, Delegation Business, Victoria, British Columbia

"*What a great resource for the small business do-it-yourself crowd! For the millions of one-person businesses -- and especially for the heavily tech-reliant, home-based business sector -- a low-jargon, tech support guide that doesn't talk down to its audience.*"
> Dawn Rivers Baker, Editor, *Wahmpreneur News Magazine*, Sidney, New York

"*Joshua's book is packed with great tips that will repay the cost of the book many, many times over -- and save endless headaches in the process. Excellent advice! Chapters are 'chunked' with great tips and advice for busy people!*"
> Brian Ward, Affinity Consulting, Edmonton, Alberta

"*Any small company will achieve an ROI from Joshua's book within the first month of buying it! I wish that I had been able to read these tricks of the trade years ago. This book would have saved time, money and gray hairs.*"
> J.R. Rodrigues, CEO, Ask A Sales Pro, Rhode Island

"*Joshua's money-saving tips are very useful to small business owners, perpetually short of cash. You'd pay good money to a consultant for this kind of advice.*"
> Hugh Anderson, Uncle Hughie's Independent Guide to Online Investing, Montreal

"*...required reading for all of our clients -- the perfect companion for any small business. If more of our clients read and followed what was in Joshua's book, it would make their lives a lot easier.*"
> Edward Crouser, Crouser & Associates, Charleston, West Virginia

"*Joshua's book contains dozens of practical tips that help business owners understand and lower their computer support costs. This book pays for itself many times over -- incredibly action-oriented!*"
> Harry Joiner, Business Development Coach, Reliable Growth

"*For the computer user who just wants to turn the thing on and go, Joshua's book is extremely useful.*"
> Shel Horowitz, Frugal Marketing, Northampton, Massachusetts

"*I'll be saving myself plenty of busywork in the future by using Joshua's easy-to-comprehend time savers.*"
> June Campbell, Nightcats Multimedia, North Vancouver, British Columbia

"*...mandatory reading for every small business owner and manager. Chock full of great money- and time-saving ideas -- technology meets the reality of the business world -- an office bible for those who want to get the most out of these monsters we call computers.*"
> William N. Hodges, DTM PDG, Hodges Seminars International, Tampa

"*...an excellent book. For the owner or office manager who doesn't want to get an IT degree, Joshua's book could easily become their bible for computing needs.*"
> Rachelle Disbennett-Lee, MS, PCC, True Direction, Aurora, Colorado

What Your Computer Consultant Doesn't Want You to Know

101 Money-Saving Secrets of Expensive Techies

Joshua Feinberg

Small Biz Tech Talk® Press

West Palm Beach, Florida

What Your Computer Consultant Doesn't Want You to Know
101 Money-Saving Secrets of Expensive Techies
By Joshua Feinberg

Published By
Small Biz Tech Talk® Press
PO Box 541958
Greenacres, FL, USA 33467
orders@smallbiztechtalk.com
www.smallbiztechtalk.com

ISBN, print ed.   0-9714153-8-2
ISBN, audio ed.   0-9714153-2-3
Printed and bound in the United States of America
Small Biz Tech Talk is a registered trademark of KISTech Communications, the parent company of Small Biz Tech Talk Press. Other company and product names mentioned in this book may be trademarks of their respective owners.

Publisher: Jennifer Feinberg
Copy Editor: Rick Garr
Cover Designer: George Foster

Publisher's Cataloging-in-Publication
(Provided by Quality Books, Inc.)

Feinberg, Joshua.
    What your computer consultant doesn't want you to know / Joshua Feinberg.
        p. cm.
        Includes bibliographical references and index.
        ISBN 0-9714153-8-2

    1. Small business--Data processing. 2. Small business--Automation. 3. Microcomputers--Purchasing. I. Title.

HF5548.2.F45 2002   658'.05
                                QBI02-200254

To the millions of small business owners and managers
who feel intimidated by all things tech

Contents

Guest Foreword

"Where was this book when I was setting up and managing my own small business computer system?" That was the one question that continually floated through my mind as I read advance pages of *What Your Computer Consultant Doesn't Want You to Know*.

As a 13-year citizen of the small business community, I've played many roles: CEO, rainmaker, customer service rep, bookkeeper – and ad hoc Information Technology (IT) manager. In my role as the go-to IT guy, those questions that were even slightly more difficult to answer than "Alt + H" (for Help!) or "when all else fails, reboot," would require a call to George, my independent tech support advisor.

And more often than not, George's information – though useful and definitive – was simple at its core. A few keystrokes, or a quick primer on troubleshooting the problem at hand, usually was all it took to resolve my issues. While the cost wasn't exorbitant, the time spent reaching this would-be sage – and asking him about what ultimately was a simple solution – would have been better spent on more profitable endeavors.

After all, time *is* money. And in the small business world, both often are in short supply. And man, don't I feel sheepish every time I bug him about something that (once it's resolved) was *so* simple that even an adolescent, on his or her first PC, could have figured it out?

In my almost 10 years of writing about small business management and IT issues, I've found that entrepreneurs take on dual roles as IT consumer *and* IT manager. The former is much revered.

When systems are running smoothly, the PC has proven itself the power tool of the small business. It allows one person or a handful of workers to multitask and perform seamlessly the functions essential to the operations of the modern business.

The latter, on the other hand, can be much reviled. When systems fail, even those small businesses with an employee overseeing IT are limited by that staffer's knowledge – or lack thereof – regarding technology and troubleshooting issues. Or, these small business owners are at the mercy of the computer consultant's availability and fee.

If I may, a quick, telling tale about IT support: A company's computer system fails. The owner calls in a consultant, who looks at the system, taps a few keys and fixes the problem on the spot. He then hands the business owner a bill for $500. The business owner is aghast. "But you only hit a few keys and fixed my problem," he pleaded. "I charge $5 for hitting the keys," the consultant said, "and $495 for knowing which keys to hit."

That's where *What Your Computer Consultant Doesn't Want You to Know* comes in. Joshua Feinberg knows which keys *you can hit* to solve your own IT problems. He has condensed more than a decade spent at IT help desks and small business back offices into 288 information-packed pages of tips, insights and plain old common sense. Just flipping through the pages I can see scores of ideas that, if implemented, will serve me well in my future computing. This book has earned its place on my reference desk beside my golden Rolodex, tattered dictionary and thesaurus. I might even call it "George."

So I ask again, "Where was this book when I was setting up and managing my own small business computer system?" Luckily for today's small business owner, "George" now comes in paperback.

Jeff Zbar
www.chiefhomeofficer.com
Small business columnist, author, advocate and speaker
U.S. Small Business Administration 2001
Small Business Journalist of the Year

Acknowledgments

I've really enjoyed writing this book. For years, small business employees, new to their part-time computer support responsibilities, have been asking me to recommend great PC how-to books, with their advanced beginner to intermediate technical level in mind.

While I've always been able to rattle off a few favorites, small business internal gurus don't have the time or luxury to read through 600 pages on Microsoft Access, notebooks or virus protection -- just to find the few bite-sized "nuggets" that are most immediately relevant to their new "job." *What Your Computer Consultant Doesn't Want You to Know* pulls together and organizes key money-saving advice, in eight distinct subject areas. I am grateful to the many people who've made this project possible.

First, a tremendous thank you goes to Jennifer Feinberg, who isn't just my wife and inspiration. She's also an extremely talented business manager, collaborator and publisher.

I'm also very grateful for the strong moral support of my sister Karen Feinberg, my parents Myra and David Feinberg, my in-laws Ann and Walt Rossler and my brother-in-law Kurt Rossler.

Several professional small business and technology colleagues gave me detailed feedback to improve the content and delivery of the book's material. As a group, these folks also made sure I was hitting the right technical level for the part-time, small business internal guru.

Thank you to Larry Lentz of Lentz Computer Services and Sid Plait of Plait Solutions – two computer consultants whose strong, positive feedback reinforced the need for and importance of this book. Deb Alloway of Free Tech Mail, small business accounting expert Gregg Bernicker, CPA, June Campbell of Nightcats Multimedia Productions, small business operations and marketing expert Susan Carter, Jeanette Cates, PhD of Tech Tamers, Peggy Duncan of the Duncan Resource Group, home business expert Paul Edwards, business columnist Jan Norman and sales trainer J.R. Rodrigues all were instrumental in reviewing advanced content and providing generous, detailed insight that helped enhance the value of *What Your Computer Consultant Doesn't Want You to Know*.

I also want to express my sincere gratitude to Hugh Anderson of Uncle Hughie's Independent Guide to Online Investing, Dawn Rivers Baker of Wahmpreneur News Magazine, Jeff Cate of PC Serv, Katherine Caughran of Delegation Business Services, Edward Crouser of Crouser & Associates, Rachelle Disbennett-Lee of True Direction, Charles Fisher of Charles L. Youngman Civil/Structural Engineering, Marty Fletcher of Chefs International, Cathy Fothergill of Connection Team, Bill Hodges of Hodges Seminars International, Shel Horowitz of Frugal Marketing, Harry Joiner of Reliable Growth, Amy Marshall of Cardre, Wayne Messick of Family Business Strategies, small business legal expert James K. Roosa, Esq., Monnie Ryan of *The Business Journal*, nationally syndicated radio and webcast host of Entrepreneurs! Tour of America Richard Tavener, Tom Tshontikidis of Ivy Sea, technology writer Andy Walker of Cyberwalker Media Syndicate and Brian Ward of Affinity Consulting.

Small business columnist, author and SOHO expert Jeff Zbar, of the Chief Home Officer and the U.S. SBA's 2001 Journalist of the Year, also provided some exceptional insight into the reach, focus, packaging, and level-balancing of *What Your Computer Consultant Doesn't Want You to Know*. Jeff also did a fantastic job on the Guest Foreword for this book.

Special thanks to our copy editor Rick Garr, who helped make the content of this book an easier read, and George Foster, our cover designer. Whoever may have told you, "you can't judge a book by its cover," knew *nothing* about the realities of the publishing industry. Everyday millions of us make split-second judgments on the value of a book based on its outward appearance. George's cover-designing talents catapulted *What Your Computer Consultant Doesn't Want You to Know* into the reaches of small businesses worldwide that can benefit from its 101 money-saving secrets.

And finally, I'd like to thank all of the small business clients and internal gurus that I've had the pleasure of working with at KISTech Computer Consulting over the years. Your questions, strong interest level and ability to absorb tech support tips, in bite-sized chunks, encouraged me to invest our resources *and* bet our business on making *you* and internal gurus around the world more self-sufficient.

Introduction

In today's information-intensive business climate, small businesses confront a number of technology challenges.

On one hand, your company needs to be *absolutely* sure it's spending its time and financial resources in the right places.

On the flip side, cutting back too much on tech expenses in the wrong places can lead to missed business opportunities, a decay in competitive positioning, abysmal employee productivity and morale as well as a high risk of severe damage to both physical and intellectual property tech assets.

Why You Need This Book Now:
Take Control of Your Technology

My goal is quite simple: to show you ways to save money on common computer support problems and related technology expenses.

To do that, I have to let you in on many insider secrets that your highly paid computer consultant doesn't want you to know. After all, the longer you're in the dark, the more billable hours your consultant can rack up on mundane tasks that very well may be within your company's scope of expertise.

Don't let another week pass in which your consultant is building up job security on your nickel, and a hefty invoice, by withholding key training and system documentation.

What Your Computer Consultant Doesn't Want You to Know will help make sure:

- Your company can begin saving money right away.

- You can provide a more immediate response to your coworkers' tech support problems. No more waiting for return phone calls, pages or on-site visits.

- You'll learn how to improve the reliability of your company's computer systems.

- You'll become a more valuable employee to your company.

- You can improve your company's individual employee and workgroup productivity.

- You'll be able to better distinguish among fact, opinion and pure fiction.

- You'll be able to figure out which tasks to continue outsourcing.

- You'll be able to support today's problems with a clear vision of what you need to accomplish down the road.

And the *best* part, these tips are organized into *simple*, bite-sized chunks for busy people.

Why This Book Is Different: The Secrets of Expensive Tech Consultants Revealed

Most conventional computer books contain a technical discussion of software features – assuming that you want *and* need to achieve expert proficiency on the topic at hand.

Computer books very rarely even touch on opportunities for cost savings, such as out-of-pocket expenses and soft costs, or training, installation, customization and troubleshooting. So you're on your own to figure out how various software and hardware features affect your technology budget. This book is *very* different.

Small business owners and managers are a price-sensitive group. So any opportunity to trim expenses, *without* cutting into muscle, is certainly worth exploring. Add 101 money-saving opportunities to the mix, and the possibilities become even more exciting.

What Your Computer Consultant Doesn't Want You to Know will help you plan innovative ways to start curtailing your technology spending almost immediately. Simply "*in*-source" many computer support projects that were formerly handled exclusively on an outsourced basis by expensive computer consultants. As you'll see, this book is truly a unique tool.

A Few Words About Tech Consultants

In my first book, *Building Profitable Solutions with Microsoft BackOffice Small Business Server 4.5* (Microsoft Press, 1999), I taught computer consultants how to constantly add high-level value to client engagements by regularly evaluating and upgrading their consulting skill sets.

I've been a long time proponent of the need for computer consultants to plan for next year's big opportunities. *Most* progressive, forward-thinking technology providers agree with this practice and actively seek ways to phase out entry-level, low-margin technical support tasks, so their companies can concentrate on higher-level projects and more lucrative niches. This gives consultants a way to combat obsolescence and build a more solid relationship and partnership with their small business clients.

But, some computer consultants out there still believe self-servingly that clients are best off being kept in the dark on self-help technical support information.

Computer consultants offer small businesses an excellent way to tap into experienced IT (Information Technology) talent, *without* the overhead of a full-time IT manager on payroll. However, many small businesses call on their computer consultant too quickly, too often, when small businesses could just as readily and easily handle many basic, routine computer support problems on their own.

If these scenarios in any way describe your existing technology provider relationship, you need *What Your Computer Consultant Doesn't Want You to Know* to help you become more self-sufficient and lower your overall computer support costs. If this sort of discussion offends your computer consultant, perhaps you should start interviewing replacements.

Who This Book Is For

- Small Business Owners, Managers and Internal Gurus

- Trusted Advisors to Small Businesses

- Technology Consultants for Small Businesses

In sharp contrast to workers in a Fortune 1000 enterprise, small business employees wear *a lot* of "hats." There are no hard and fast rules on when a small business *must* put an IT manager on payroll, but with fewer than 25 PC users, it's difficult to rationalize or cost-justify having a full-time salaried computer support position.

So daily computer support tasks and ongoing tech projects typically are handled part-time by an employee who has another job with the company, call it his or her "real" job -- such as being an accountant, bookkeeper, controller, executive assistant, office manager, sales rep or some other *non*-IT career. I call this person the *internal guru* – the one everybody instinctively yells for when the fax machine jams, the Internet connection goes down or the database locks up.

In addition to the internal guru, many small businesses have a "P&L" decision maker, responsible for the firm's **Profit & Loss** Statement, who presides over the more strategic, financial decisions of which technology projects merit investment. Sometimes the internal guru, acting in a tactical or operations capacity, is authorized to sign off on *all* related financial decisions. However, often an owner or high-level manager such as a controller or CFO, is actively involved with the *major* financial decisions on technology spending and ultimately signs the related contracts and purchase orders.

Although this book is built around the needs of both the small business internal guru and the P&L decision maker, at least two *major* constituencies of professional service providers who work with small businesses also can benefit tremendously from the subjects explored here.

- **Trusted Advisors to Small Businesses** – such as Certified Public Accountants (CPAs) and their equivalent outside the USA, management consultants, attorneys and financial planners

- **Technology Consultants for Small Businesses** – such as Application Service Providers (ASPs), computer consultants, integrators, Internet Service Providers (ISPs), Independent Software Vendors (ISVs) and Value Added Resellers (VARs)

Although this book emphasizes cost-reduction issues, it is *not* a substitute for the sound advice of other trusted small business advisors. Before implementing any major changes to your company based on suggestions in this book, check with an appropriate small business resource such as your accountant, attorney, financial planner or management consultant.

What Your Computer Consultant Doesn't Want You to Know is consciously a PC-centric book and assumes that the reader is largely committed to Intel-based desktop PCs, notebook PCs and servers, Microsoft Windows operating systems and the Microsoft Office productivity suite. Because of their limited following among small businesses relative to the above market-share desktop dominators, only minimal discussion is made of alternative products such as the Apple Mac OS and Linux.

Most of this book deals with the desktop and notebook PC side of the network, with limited discussion of server and networking issues. Because most small business internal gurus are approaching their part-time IT responsibilities with only a limited amount of time in a given week, their scarce resources are best spent first concentrating on the simplest technologies and surrounding issues.

Although monetary estimates in this book are listed in U.S. dollars, the majority of this book is applicable to both U.S.-based *and* international small businesses.

How This Book Is Organized: 101 Tips – Bite-Sized Chunks of Powerful Knowledge

What Your Computer Consultant Doesn't Want You to Know is based on dozens of related computer support topics and challenges faced by most small businesses.

The tips are presented as easy-to-digest, well-organized nuggets of knowledge you can refer to over and over again, as needed.

Each tip provides either an opportunity to save money on a direct technology expense or the background to mitigate a soft cost, such as the time spent on a given task. In addition, many tips warn of potential pitfalls.

In Part I, Hardware Cost-Saving Tips, we'll dive right into more than 40 money-saving tips on common PC hardware issues with desktop PCs, notebook PCs and servers (Chapter 1). Then, in Chapter 2, we'll concentrate on two PC peripheral devices that can cause an astonishing amount of support headaches: modems and printers.

In Part II, Software Cost-Saving Tips, we'll shift our attention to money-saving opportunities with Microsoft Office (Chapter 3) and Microsoft Windows (Chapter 4). We'll round out our look at software with Software Purchases and Maintenance in Chapter 5.

Part III, Data Protection Cost-Saving Tips, is all about reducing costs by protecting your company's information assets from the "bad guys" and various other significant risks. First we'll delve into saving your data from malicious and accidental losses in Data Backup (Chapter 6). Next, we'll survey techniques to prevent your computers from getting fried by utility power damage or your data from getting zapped out of existence (Chapter 7). Then, we'll wrap up in Chapter 8 with an overview of virus prevention techniques.

At the conclusion of *What Your Computer Consultant Doesn't Want You to Know*, you'll find a comprehensive glossary that pulls together more than 160 terms used throughout the book and contains both extensive cross-references and chapter references. There's also a consolidated resource directory recapping suggested Web sites.

You'll not only learn how to achieve world-class tech results on a small business budget, but you'll also gain a much better understanding of how to approach many common computer support issues –

without always having to call in an expensive professional computer consultant.

Cost-Saving Emphasis

Each tip begins with a summary of whether you can expect to save money on soft costs, out-of-pocket expenses, or both.

✓ **Save on Soft Costs**

✓ **Save on Out-of-Pocket Expenses**

Soft costs are any expenses that *cannot* be directly accounted for and itemized as out-of-pocket expenses for product and service purchases. In addition to installation, configuration and troubleshooting, soft costs encompass needs analysis, product selection, procurement, testing, customization, training, documentation, ongoing maintenance and upgrading.

Out-of-pocket expenses are *much* easier to quantify as direct product or service purchases – such as buying a desktop PC, monitor, modem or a year of Web site hosting.

In areas where alternative solutions are presented, you'll find a **Relative Cost Indicator**, in addition to a discussion of each solution's pros and cons.

$ **Least Expensive**

$$ **Moderately Expensive**

$$$ **A Major Investment**

$$$$ **Over the Top for Most Small Businesses**

What You Should Already Know

What Your Computer Consultant Doesn't Want You to Know is written primarily for the small business internal guru: someone whose IT endeavors are basically part-time and sustained with little, if any, formal classroom training on hardware, software or networking.

Many of the people who can benefit from this book often don't give themselves enough credit for as much as they *do* know about computers.

If you've picked up this book and feel comfortable using a PC, Microsoft Windows, Microsoft Office and a Web browser, you *can* learn a great deal from *What Your Computer Consultant Doesn't Want You to Know*.

And, better yet, you're already well on your way to becoming a more effective, cost-scrutinizing internal guru!

My Unique Circumstances That Made This Book Possible

Since 1989, I've been in the trenches supporting thousands of PC users, as well as their peripherals, software applications, operating systems, network environments and unique configuration choices. *What Your Computer Consultant Doesn't Want You to Know* is based on my years of observing these best practices among small business PC users.

Several years ago, I started to notice a trend among many of the local internal gurus I trained. During each service call at a client site, I always spent 15 to 20 minutes providing some kind of highly-targeted hands-on training for the internal guru. Over the course of 20 to 30 site visits in a given year, these internal gurus became *remarkably* self-sufficient – almost rivaling a full-time, junior systems administrator. My unique approach cemented client relationships, leading to incredible amounts of loyalty, while freeing me up from basic how-to questions so I could concentrate on true high-level consulting.

In 1997, I began writing a series of monthly columns called *Small Business Smarts* for a trade magazine read by computer resellers worldwide, *Selling Windows NT Solutions*, as well as their parent publication, *Windows NT Magazine*. Shortly thereafter, as a contributing editor I started getting e-mail from both U.S. and international technology consultants. E-mail after e-mail validated the same trend: technology providers felt strongly that training internal gurus was an integral part of any successful small business project.

In 1999, I was hired by the Microsoft Corporation to create and produce an online bi-weekly column for small business technology providers. With a circulation approaching seven figures and translations into more than a dozen languages, my *Notes from the Field* articles confirmed in even greater volumes that small business internal gurus *desperately* needed more targeted training.

In 2001, I launched Small Biz Tech Talk to show small businesses directly how to save money on computer support costs. This book is the culmination of my years of experience as a small business technology expert.

My Pledge to You

In this easy-to-navigate guide, you'll learn to outsource less and *in*source more. So next time, you won't need to call an expensive outside consultant when approaching a routine or relatively simple-to-grasp tech problem.

You'll discover how to tackle everyday, repetitive, relatively low-risk computer support tasks on your own, as well as field-tested techniques to become more self-sufficient.

You'll also see lots of opportunities to leverage existing employees to successfully bring many computer support functions back "in house." These are the tips, hints and insider secrets that many highly paid computer consultants don't want you to know.

Feedback

I hope you enjoy reading this book as much as I enjoyed writing it. My even greater hope is that you use the advice and tools in *What Your Computer Consultant Doesn't Want You to Know* to lower your computer support expenses and become more self-sufficient.

Best of luck and keep in touch! I'd love to hear from you. Drop me a line at letters@smallbiztechtalk.com and let me know how you're making out with your company's tech support tasks.

All the best,

Joshua Feinberg
Small Biz Tech Talk
West Palm Beach, Florida, USA
www.smallbiztechtalk.com

Part I

Hardware Cost-Saving Tips

Chapter 1
PC Hardware Purchases

Desktops, Notebooks, Servers,
Hardware Selection, Bundled Components,
Vendor Tech Support and Warranty Issues

Smart PC hardware selection can make your installation, support, troubleshooting and upgrading work *much* easier. Selecting the right PCs and related peripherals can lower your company's computer support costs *dramatically*, while boosting system reliability and employee productivity. Pick the wrong PC hardware and well let's not even go there!

Despite all the advances during the past few years, the venerable desktop, notebook and server have remained the staples of the PC hardware world. Sure, there are newcomers. Since the mid-'90s, both Palm and Microsoft have spearheaded competing handheld standards. And now there are special-purpose rack-mountable servers, with surely more to come, dedicated to the unique demands of serving high-volume Web sites.

We'll start this chapter with a look at cost reduction techniques for desktop PCs, notebook computers and, to a lesser extent, servers. Then, we'll examine computer support and cost considerations with product warranties, component upgrades and spare parts. In Chapter 2, we'll highlight computer support cost concerns for various peripherals, primarily modems and printers, as well as related underlying hardware technologies.

Tip #1

Don't be the first on the block to buy something new, *unless* you have a really good reason *and* can cost-justify it.

Save on Soft Costs

✓ **Save on Out-of-Pocket Expenses**

Buying the latest and greatest PC, whether it's a desktop, notebook or server, is a lot like purchasing a new car at the beginning of the model year, as soon as it becomes available. Sure, you'll get the fastest processor, the most RAM and the slickest supporting components. However, you'll pay a steep price for the novelty of being an early adopter.

People always ask me, "So Josh, what's the difference between the high-end $2,100 desktop PC and the entry-level $599 desktop PC?" At the risk of oversimplifying matters, think of the entry-level $599 PC as last year's model, or what you might've spent $2,100 on just one short year ago.

So you're paying an enormous premium for being first on the block to own a state-of-the-art PC. As a result, your small business may incur massive depreciation expenses – much like the way a new car loses several thousand dollars in book value the moment you drive it off the dealer's lot. Because these expenses are rarely trivial, start things off right by keeping new PC purchases under close watch. And don't be shy about seeking out bona fide bargains on last year's model whenever possible.

Note:
You can apply similar logic to purchases of new notebook computers and servers. However, a notebook or server, *other things being equal*, almost always will be more expensive than a desktop PC.

If you're looking to keep abreast of special promotions and other PC bargains, check out the following Web sites.

- **CNET Shopper** -- www.shopper.com

- **eBay** -- www.ebay.com

- **TechBargains** -- www.techbargains.com

Tip #2

But don't skimp on power users who run high-end software.

✓ **Save on Soft Costs**

✓ **Save on Out-of-Pocket Expenses**

On the flip side of the coin, don't lump all of your employees together when you analyze PC hardware requirements. Many small office employees depend mainly on software with modest hardware requirements, such as basic word processing, spreadsheet, e-mail and Web browsing software. However, there are certainly exceptions. Make sure *you* know who your company's power users are.

If your small business depends on an advanced software application, such as graphics design, computer assisted design (CAD) or financial modeling, it may be advisable to implicitly eat that sky-high first year's depreciation on the purchase of the latest and greatest PC hardware. With processor and memory-intensive software applications, the employee productivity your company will gain with leading-edge PC hardware likely will offset any major depreciation cost concerns.

Also consider the salary required to attract and retain highly technical professionals who run advanced software applications. For example, if you have a veteran graphic design artist on your payroll at a $60,000 base salary, you'd be foolish to hinder the designer's productivity with an entry-level PC. An extra $1,000 a year on PC-related expenses for this designer *easily* could drive a productivity gain that makes the incremental expense seem trivial.

Note:
In many small businesses, the premium performance PC purchased for the power user gets replaced every year or two, and is passed down to an end user with less demanding software requirements. This is one way to extend the life of an expensive, high-end PC, while minimizing the out-of-pocket and related support expenses of bringing new PC hardware into your company.

Tip #3

Avoid letting egos influence your PC purchase decisions.

Save on Soft Costs

✓ **Save on Out-of-Pocket Expenses**

The temptation is great to outfit your top managers and producers with the latest and greatest PC hardware. After all, a CFO or senior account manager has a *tremendous* amount riding on his or her daily performance and productivity.

Basic Business Applications

However, look carefully at software application requirements before emotional needs drive tech purchases.

If your CFO spends most of a typical day crunching numbers in Microsoft Excel spreadsheets and communicating via e-mail in Microsoft Outlook, he or she really has very basic PC requirements.

Notebook Gadget Black Holes

Pay particular attention to notebooks. You can get some really useful multimedia features in high-end notebooks in the $4,000 to $5,000 price range.

But if the owner of the company merely wants to access e-mail remotely, you *easily* could equip him or her with a reliable, high-performance, brand-name notebook for one-third to one-half of that price range.

Don't allow your objective judgment and technology budget to get seduced by superfluous bells and whistles.

Tip #4

Don't let a budget surplus burn a hole in your pocket or drive up PC support costs.

✓ **Save on Soft Costs**

Save on Out-of-Pocket Expenses

I began my career, more than a decade ago, selling PC hardware to large colleges, universities and school districts.

In the educational world, as in many government entities, there's a use-it-or-lose-it budgeting philosophy that permeates the purchase of PC-related products.

Use It or Lose It

So, for example, if you're the science department chairperson for a local school district, and you have a $500,000 budget this year for computer products, you "need" to spend it.

What are the consequences of *not* spending your total technology budget?

For starters, any funds left over will *not* carry forward to next year. And, the board of education probably will believe your department no longer needs the full annual $500,000 budget for computer products.

Your department's allocation likely will be reduced going forward. So there's a year-end rush to deplete the technology budget account, regardless of whether the timing is right for getting the best purchase value or controlling computer support costs.

All too often, small businesses fall into a similar trap, ignoring the entrepreneurial instincts that got them on the map in the first place. Don't feel that just because you're having a "great" year, quarter or month, that you need to buy *every* PC gadget and gizmo you've ever dreamed of having or heard someone gushing about.

Good Mood Buying Binges

Along the same lines, resist the temptation to compress all of your PC-related purchases into a brief window, when the owner of the company may be in a good mood and approachable about technology spending.

Cost-effective use of small business technology comes about through detailed planning and execution.

Heading down to the warehouse club or local office supply super-store and splurging impulsively on a $20,000 computer shopping spree with your corporate credit card may *feel* good.

But without proper planning, these sudden tech asset purchases actually may increase your company's computer support costs.

The purchase price of hardware and software is only a fraction of what these assets cost your company to own and operate.

You need to consider all the related expenses, such as installation, customization, training, support, troubleshooting, maintenance and upgrading, as well as many other related soft costs.

Tip:
Be sure to carefully research how your PC vendor handles warranty service and technical support. Both areas are discussed later in this chapter and can have a *huge* impact on your computer support costs.

Tip #5

Reallocate your PC hardware budget to get the greatest impact.

✓ **Save on Soft Costs**

✓ **Save on Out-of-Pocket Expenses**

If your recent financial results have been *so* spectacular that you feel now is *the* time to make significant technology investments in your company, consider the following.

Budget Surplus

You could reallocate the surplus funds for something else technology-related that you *really* need. This could be end user or administrator training, so your company can get more out of your PC hardware, software and networking investments. Planned wisely, training will do wonders to reduce your computer support costs and boost employee productivity.

You also could earmark the budget surplus for upgrading and replacing PCs more regularly. Because entry-level PCs are often one-half to two-thirds less expensive than top-of-the-line models, you'll still be way ahead of the game. Just don't forget to factor in a few hours of configuration time for each PC upgrade, from an older to a newer PC.

Alternatively, maybe now's a good time to upgrade your Internet access to boost its performance and dependability. Again, how you finagle your tech budget and related investments is a *very* individualized decision, but think big picture and don't be afraid to break tradition.

Investment Mindset

Also, note here that I begin to use the word "investment" in this book. You must think about your PC-related purchases not just as one-time expenses *but* as traceable investments. And, as any capital expenditure, well-thought-out PC hardware purchases should provide a positive return on investment (ROI).

Don't think of your PCs as office equipment. Your PC-related assets have a *much* greater impact on the success or failure of your business than a fax machine, photocopy machine, filing cabinet or water cooler. Technology investments can make or break a small business. So before you contemplate *any* major purchase, think about the cost *and* the benefits, as well as how you'll measure these benefits.

29

Tip #6

Don't become your PC vendor's science experiment.

✓ **Save on Soft Costs**

Save on Out-of-Pocket Expenses

If the first year's depreciation cost of purchasing the latest and greatest PC hardware doesn't deter you, this might. If your company purchases a PC with a processor that's just been released, a new kind of motherboard, a revolutionary kind of graphics accelerator or updated chipset, you may get some unpleasant surprises.

Early Adopter Risks

As the PC industry continues to experience unprecedented financial pressures, a *lot* more products will be rushed to market.

In early 2001, leading IT market research firm Gartner Dataquest announced that the U.S. PC market shrank by 3.5 percent, compared to the same period a year earlier. This was the first industry contraction in seven years.

One only can wonder if as the hardware giants reduce headcount, expenses and R&D, will consumers become an extended R&D facility? This revelation is really nothing new to the PC industry.

For at least a decade, PC owners and small businesses have had to grapple with a continuous stream of updated hardware device driver software and reprogrammable firmware updates.

The trouble is, from the time problems are first reported, analyzed, diagnosed and ultimately fixed through updates, *someone* has to suffer with unreliable hardware products. If you're looking to control computer support costs, you don't want to be your hardware vendor's guinea pig.

Lots of Windows

There's one more variable to consider in all this: operating systems. I *cannot* recall a time in recent memory when anywhere near six current generation mainstream operating systems were on the market, *and* that's just from Microsoft.

PC hardware vendors need to support everything including Microsoft Windows 95, Windows NT 4, Windows 98, Windows 2000, Windows Millennium Edition (Me) and Windows XP.

Glossary:
Have you visited this book's Glossary yet? Get a quick refresher on over 160 terms used throughout this book -- all those buzzwords and acronyms frequently thrown around by computer consultants and other techies. The Glossary, with extensive cross-references and chapter references, begins on page 231.

Now if six versions of Microsoft Windows weren't enough, consider all the service releases and service packs that accompany the products. So you easily can see why there is *so* much potential for major headaches with PC hardware-induced computer support problems.

One simple way to avoid most of this aggravation: Don't be the first to jump at new products.

Companion CD-ROM

Are you ready to take your cost-savings to the next level, but you're at a loss for the *right* questions to ask? Check out the Companion CD-ROM for *What Your Computer Consultant Doesn't Want You to Know* -- with over 550 Action Items to get you started saving money right now.

The Action Items are presented in a variety of convenient file formats including Adobe Acrobat .pdf, HTML, Microsoft Word .doc and Microsoft Excel .xls. In addition, the Action Items are loaded up in a Microsoft Outlook Personal Folders File (.pst) -- ready for you to import into your Microsoft Outlook Tasks. The Companion CD-ROM also includes an electronic Resource Directory, recapping the book's suggested Web sites, that's all set for you to import into your Microsoft Internet Explorer Favorites list. Use the handy Action Item format to copy, paste and delegate -- while you tailor the money-saving program to your company's unique needs.

For more information on the Companion CD-ROM, see page 285.

Or visit www.smallbiztechtalk.com/tools/ to download sample Action Items or order the Companion CD-ROM.

Tip #7

Select a small business PC.

✓ **Save on Soft Costs**

✓ **Save on Out-of-Pocket Expenses**

In the early to mid-'90s, leading PC vendors began segmenting their product lines into two or three distinct tiers.

As the domestic and global market demand for desktop PCs, notebooks and servers began to soar, top PC vendors such as Compaq, Dell, Gateway, Hewlett Packard and IBM wanted to have PC products that would be highly relevant and compelling for various needs and budgets.

- **Enterprise customers**, such as Fortune 1000 network managers, would pay premium prices but require incredible amounts of scalability, reliability and availability, stable and mature hardware configurations, as well as ease of manageability. *Relative Cost Indicator*: $$$

- **Home users** would need rock-bottom prices to entice first-time buyers, as well as bleeding edge hardware components for gaming, digital photography, video capture and other Internet-era hobbies. *Relative Cost Indicator*: $

- **Small business** users would need something in between -- not too stripped down, not too loaded up, but a very good mid-range value. *Relative Cost Indicator*: $$

Fortunately, the PC vendors also have made identifying appropriate products easier. When shopping for a PC online, PC vendors' Web sites almost always will have separate Web pages and sections for each of these three market segments. This helps to make sure you inadvertently don't buy a PC with the wrong set of features.

Tip #8

Choose the right PC specs to save big money on unpredictable installation and support costs.

✓ **Save on Soft Costs**

✓ **Save on Out-of-Pocket Expenses**

Although promoted PC configurations change daily and weekly, there are some must have and some recommended optional line items to look for when you purchase a small business PC.

In a perfect world, all software and hardware vendors claiming compatibility, under a particular operating system or PC environment, would have products that work well together. But, this *isn't* a perfect world.

You can save yourself considerable time and potential aggravation, and pick up substantial out-of-pocket savings, by getting various hardware components and software programs *preinstalled* with the purchase of a new PC.

In much the same way that you'll often find greater overall value by getting more menu items bundled into a complete dinner at a restaurant, such as when a meal includes soup, salad, beverage or dessert, there are *many* times when it makes small business sense to purchase various hardware components and upgrades with the purchase of the PC -- as opposed to shopping for these hardware components and upgrades a la carte at a later date. And we're not just talking about out-of-pocket cost savings. There is *huge* potential soft cost savings as well.

Note:
Tip #9 through Tip #12 provide details on developing your PC purchase specification list.

Tip #9

Purchase the video monitor with your desktop PC.

✓ **Save on Soft Costs**

✓ **Save on Out-of-Pocket Expenses**

Although there are really no major compatibility issues to consider between PCs and monitors, most PC vendors offer good deals on monitors purchased with PCs.

For due diligence, always price the PC with *and* without the monitor, to see what you're actually paying. Then look to see whether that monitor price is in line with purchasing a *comparable* monitor separate from the PC. However, there's an even greater consideration.

When purchasing the monitor along with your desktop PC, the monitor warranty generally is incorporated into any on-site warranty coverage with the PC. That means, if your monitor needs replacement during the on-site warranty period, your PC vendor usually will arrange to cross-ship a replacement monitor.

This provides a few very compelling benefits.

- **No need to store and retain packing materials** -- You don't have to worry that you've thrown away the box and packing materials for the monitor. There's no need to purchase return shipping supplies as you'll be able to return the broken monitor in the same box your replacement comes in.

- **Save time with freight logistics** -- You don't have to locate a shipping outlet. In most cases, the PC vendor includes return shipping labels (call tags) for a specific freight carrier – generally the same freight carrier used for shipping the replacement to you.

- **Save money on freight costs** -- If the PC vendor supplies return shipping labels, you won't have to pay for return freight. Depending on the monitor size, origination and destination shipping points, this *easily* can save you $25 or more.

That third bullet point affects direct out-of-pocket costs, but the first two can be labor-intensive chores for your internal computer administrator ("internal guru") or small business computer consultant.

So buying a monitor along with a PC, and getting both purchases folded into on-site warranty coverage, easily can save a half-hour to an hour (or more) *every* time a monitor needs replacement.

What's the "best" monitor size for a small business PC?

The best value today tends to be standard 17" and 19" CRT-based monitors, with 21" monitors and flat screen LCD panel displays rapidly approaching attractive small business price points. Even if your office space is cramped, or you have a very limited budget, there are some definite productivity reasons to steer clear of any monitor smaller than 17".

With a 17" monitor, most people configure their video display adapter for an 800-by-600 pixel resolution. This allows you to get substantially more content onto your screen, *without* eyestrain, than on a 14" or 15" monitor running at a lower video resolution setting.

To configure video display adapter settings of 1,024-by-768 pixel resolution, the next popular upgrade from 800-by-600 pixels, you'd likely want a 19" monitor. Some people prefer to squeeze more onto a screen, but frankly that makes me squint.

Others with very poor eyesight may prefer less information on the screen and larger displays. This alternative is the equivalent of large-print books for the visually impaired.

Generally, the more you see on the monitor simultaneously, the less scrolling you'll need to do. This ultimately helps you get more work done faster -- less time scrolling means more time to be productive.

Tip #10

Purchase a CD-RW drive with a PC.

✓ **Save on Soft Costs**

✓ **Save on Out-of-Pocket Expenses**

A CD-RW drive is a mass storage device that can hold the equivalent of several hundred diskettes on very inexpensive, removable media.

Unlike a video monitor, an *internal* CD-RW storage device gets installed *inside* your desktop PC. On a notebook, the CD-RW drive is generally either built-in, or installed in a modular bay *and* "swappable" for either a diskette drive, second hard drive or additional battery.

Bundled vs. a la Carte

Regardless of whether you're considering a desktop PC or notebook, there are *definite* compatibility issues to be concerned with between a CD-RW drive, the accompanying operating system and other hardware components.

With a notebook, you're generally restricted to proprietary parts that *only* work with a particular brand, make and model of notebook. So if you want an internal CD-RW drive, you'll probably need the sole supported brand and model from the notebook manufacturer.

With a desktop PC, you have many more options for adding a CD-RW drive. You *could* purchase an internal CD-RW drive later and install it yourself. But, it's *much* simpler to get the CD-RW drive at the same time. By having the CD-RW drive factory installed, you know it will work with your PC and operating system. No guesswork. No tedious calls to technical support. Minimal, if any frustration.

Adding a CD-RW drive to a notebook later presents fewer compatibility and installation challenges. Nevertheless, buying the CD-RW drive from the same PC vendor later still may mean you're getting a newer CD-RW drive than was intended for your notebook – possibly exposing you to configuration hassles.

Resource Directory:
Want an easy way to recall the over 60 Web site references discussed in this book? Check out the Resource Directory, starting on page 261, for suggested Web sites that deal with PC hardware and peripherals, software applications and operating systems, data protection and other general small business technology information.

Tech Support and Warranty Issues

The PC vendor who bundled the CD-RW drive with the desktop PC or notebook purchase also *should* stand behind the configuration as "supported," if and when you need to call for assistance. This one-stop shopping approach also can prove invaluable, as you won't be subjected to the all-too-typical finger-pointing and accountability shirking between a component manufacturer and a PC vendor.

There are warranty-related benefits as well. The bundled CD-RW drive will be covered by your PC's warranty. This will provide similar soft cost benefits to those discussed earlier in the context of video monitors.

Finally, the incremental cost of upgrading from a standard CD-ROM drive to a CD-RW drive at time of purchase is usually minimal.

Note:

Although CD-RW drives are a great, inexpensive, universal way to archive and backup a few hundred megabytes (MBs) of data, you also should consider risks. For example, if security is not properly configured on your network, a CD-RW drive could provide an easy way to pilfer data, just as a diskette drive can be used for similar purposes – on a *much* smaller scale. In addition, if your software installation CDs aren't locked up, a CD-RW drive could be used to pirate software media.

Tip #11

Purchase a network card with a PC.

✓ **Save on Soft Costs**

✓ **Save on Out-of-Pocket Expenses**

In the past, you probably would care only about getting an Ethernet network adapter factory installed if you knew you needed to plug your desktop PC or notebook into your office's local area network (LAN). However, in the past few years, even home PC users typically need a network adapter for connecting to broadband Internet access services provided through cable modem service and DSL (digital subscriber line).

Even if the cost of buying an Ethernet adapter a la carte was the same as the bundled price, you still should get your Ethernet adapter with your PC purchase for largely the same reasons as the CD-RW drive.

You won't need to worry about compatibility between your Ethernet adapter, other hardware components in your PC and your operating system. All device driver installation and configuration hassles are already taken care of for you.

You'll also have an easier time getting help from your PC vendor's technical support department. Plus your PC vendor will recognize the Ethernet adapter as part of the complete system and "supported" configuration.

And, once again, the Ethernet adapter likely will be covered under your standard system warranty.

Note:
In many cases, Ethernet adapters are being built into the PC motherboards on desktop PCs and notebooks. Thus, there is no explicit option to include or exclude the Ethernet adapter. It just appears on the PC motherboard like a serial or parallel port. The only downside is that, if your Ethernet adapter breaks, the PC manufacturer will need to replace your entire motherboard. If this happens after your warranty period has ended, you usually can disable the onboard Ethernet adapter and install a third-party Ethernet adapter in an available PCI or PCMCIA expansion slot.

Tip #12

Don't buy a hardware component on your own if you can get a comparable or better deal from your PC vendor.

✓ **Save on Soft Costs**

✓ **Save on Out-of-Pocket Expenses**

How can PC vendors afford to include all these bundled hardware components for *so* little money?

Consider the sheer economies of scale. You go down to the local warehouse club or office supply superstore to buy a few Ethernet network adapters. You pay a respectable price and get the product in a pretty package with a full-color box, installation guide, installation media and a vague promise of vendor technical support.

Now consider a purchasing manager for a *huge* PC vendor such as Compaq or Dell. The purchasing manager approaches that same manufacturer of Ethernet network adapters and negotiates a volume price for procuring 100,000 or more of these *every* month. And by the way, the Ethernet network adapter manufacturer won't need to supply fancy retail, shrink-wrapped boxes, installation guides or media. And the *huge* PC vendor will provide all the technical support.

Quite obviously, the giant PC vendor will get a *much* better deal than you or I could ever hope for at the retail, or even "perceived" wholesale level. Now extrapolate the discussion out to monitors, hard drives, RAM, operating systems, software applications and more, and you begin to see how the *huge* PC vendors can include these bundled items for such a low incremental cost.

So take advantage of as many of these bundled product offers as you possibly can. They tend to be *fabulous* values.

Note:

In Chapter 5, we'll discuss software programs you can get bundled with the purchase of a new small business desktop PC or notebook. The top PC vendors generally bundle operating systems, office automation applications and utility programs.

Tip #13

Find out what kind of vendor support is included with your PC purchase.

✓ **Save on Soft Costs**

Save on Out-of-Pocket Expenses

Rather than get an unpleasant surprise when you need help the most, get the lowdown on vendor technical support options *before* you make the purchase decision.

Although many top PC vendors have *similar* capabilities and services, ask about included technical support services, and preferably get a description of them in writing. Here's why.

> Good vendor technical support can save you *big* money on computer support costs.

Now, please read that last sentence again, this time out loud.

Highlight it with a yellow marker and put a reminder note on your computer monitor about the critical importance of this vendor selection requirement.

And don't forget the flip side. Lame, misguided or difficult-to-reach vendor technical support can cost your company *dearly.*

Regardless of whether your internal guru handles most PC hardware troubleshooting, you outsource those tasks to a local computer consultant or use some combination of the two, your company *will* need vendor technical support resources. No matter how smart you think you are, or how experienced you are at PC hardware troubleshooting, calling on a specialist is a necessity sometimes.

Table of Tips:
Need a quick refresher on the 101 money-saving tips discussed in this book? Check out the Table of Tips, beginning on page 267, for a chapter-by-chapter recap and quick reference.

Reaching the Specialist

Case in point: In the past decade, I must have installed more than 500 APC battery backup (UPS) devices. However, every once in a while, I still need to place a call to APC's technical support group.

As a small business technology coach, I'm more like the general practice physician -- knowing a little about a lot of different areas.

But when I'm stumped or have a technical question on a specific product, I want direct access to a specialist who deals with nothing but that particular product all day. Usually, my only regret was that I didn't pick up the phone or visit the equivalent online resource sooner.

Most important, gather your information about included technical support options *before* you make your PC purchase decision or, at the very latest, *before* you have a dire PC-related hardware emergency that requires urgent attention.

Tip:

PC *Magazine* (www.pcmag.com) regularly evaluates PC vendors' technical support quality.

Tip #14

Get the details on included and optional warranty coverage *before* you make the purchase decision.

✓ **Save on Soft Costs**

Save on Out-of-Pocket Expenses

Nearly all PC hardware vendors provide some form of product warranty. However, not all warranties are created equal.

Most reputable vendors stand behind their products, *but* each PC vendor seems to have a unique way of defining these commitments.

Although most warranty policies provide for both parts and labor, on some items labor coverage may be completely irrelevant.

For example, if your mouse, keyboard or monitor needs replacement, the vendor simply will provide the part. In most cases, you won't need a technician to visit to replace an external failed part.

Because of the high cost of dispatching a factory-trained technician to your office, PC vendors often try to get you to agree to perform your own parts replacement – even on internal components. (Say for example, a diskette or CD-RW drive fails on your desktop PC.)

In many cases, the PC vendor will overnight you the part to replace yourself, with the offer of phone support if you need assistance while replacing the failed part. If you're squeamish about this prospect, ask about vendors policies now, instead of finding out during a system crisis.

Tip #15

Ask how warranty service is handled for hard drive replacement.

✓ **Save on Soft Costs**

✓ **Save on Out-of-Pocket Expenses**

What kinds of labor are covered if a desktop PC or notebook hard drive needs replacement under the warranty?

Although warranty service almost never includes data restoration, vendor PC warranty policies vary widely.

Only Half the Job Covered

Some vendors specify that the hard drive device needs to be just physically replaced and operational, and recognized by the PC hardware setup program. Under this form of warranty coverage, the technician's job is done the moment the empty (blank) replacement hard drive is installed in your PC.

This means you're on your own to reinstall and configure the operating system, device drivers, as well as any software applications or utility programs that originally were bundled with the PC.

If you've never done this kind of project before, be especially prepared for anywhere from several hours of work to a near impossible feat, if you don't have the relevant installation media and product unlock keys.

The Real Cost

Unfortunately, as most PC vendors feel financial pressure to reduce their support and warranty costs, you probably will be subjected to this no-frills warranty service approach.

Hard drives for desktop PCs are relatively inexpensive, around $100 to $200 at retail. So it's important to understand that the warranty service on a hard drive replacement generally doesn't cover the more substantial labor costs involved with restoring the hard drive and system to the pre-crash condition.

If you outsource the task to a professional computer consultant, it easily could cost you $200 to $500 (or more) in labor to get that PC hard drive back to its pre-crash condition. Even if your internal guru handles the work, this easily could pull your internal guru away from his or her real job for a half-day or more.

Because the expense of recovering a crashed desktop PC hard drive tends to be more concentrated on soft costs, which most times aren't covered by the PC vendor's warranty anyway, we see more and more reason *not* to purchase extended warranty coverage with entry-level desktop PCs. This favors the self-insurance approach on desktop PC extended warranties, covered in Tip #18, under Spare Desktop PCs.

Note:
Because of extreme costs, business interruptions and inconveniences of a hard drive crash, you'll want to take lots of precautions to prevent this sort of outcome in the first place. For an overview of data protection techniques that can save you money, see Part III.

Tip #16
Scrutinize notebook PC warranties.

✓ **Save on Soft Costs**

✓ **Save on Out-of-Pocket Expenses**

With notebooks, individual hardware components are *much* more specialized than components used for desktop PCs. For example, notebook hard drives are not so generic as desktop PC hard drives.

Parts Not so Common

You'd probably be unable to buy a replacement notebook hard drive locally at a warehouse club or office supply superstore. And even if you miraculously could find one, the price likely would be at least double the cost of a comparable desktop PC hard drive. As a result, the value of hardware component warranty coverage on a notebook is *substantially* greater.

Unlike desktop PC hard drive replacements, notebook hard drive replacements can be expensive, both from a soft cost perspective as well as the cost of the actual replacement part. Moreover, because notebooks require specific parts, it's pretty difficult to quickly obtain appropriate replacement parts on your own.

Extended Warranty Rationale

In sharp contrast to warranty options on desktop PCs, you'll really want to purchase the maximum extended warranty coverage you can with a new notebook. Even beyond a potential hard drive failure on a notebook, consider the cost of replacing the LCD screen.

Unlike a conventional PC monitor, notebook LCD screens are highly specialized for particular notebooks. If you needed to replace a standard 17" or 19" monitor that's out of warranty, you'd generally have no problem finding equivalent products at local retail outlets for relatively modest prices of about $200 to $300.

For a notebook LCD screen, you'd almost never find the parts locally. And the LCD screen, related assembly and cable purchased separately easily could run $1,000 or more. So because of the risks of hard drive and LCD screen failures on a notebook, buying an extended service plan becomes a no-brainer. This is also the primary reason extended warranties on notebooks cost a *lot* more than comparable extended warranties on desktop PCs.

Tip #17

Consider notebook warranty upgrades.

✓ **Save on Soft Costs**

✓ **Save on Out-of-Pocket Expenses**

If you're buying an extended service plan for a new notebook, be sure to get a written statement detailing what's included and *not* included.

Unfortunately, PC vendors won't always tell you specifically what's *not* included. Sometimes, you'll only be able to surmise what's missing by comparing written warranty statements from different PC vendors.

Hazard Coverage

For example, most notebook vendors specifically exclude warranty claims arising from obvious neglect issues, such as spilling liquid on a notebook or dropping the notebook. Other notebook vendors, for a hefty price, may cover such calamities under limited circumstances.

Also consider whether you'll be traveling with your notebook. Unlike your desktop PC, which likely will stay relatively stationary throughout its life cycle, your notebook probably will go on the road with you.

International Coverage

Some notebook vendors include international warranty coverage in the base price of the extended warranty. Others charge extra for this supplemental coverage. Regardless, if you travel abroad, be sure to ask about specifics.

Just as with a desktop PC, find out whether the notebook extended warranty is on-site, where the technician comes to you, or whether you'll need to ship your notebook back to a service depot for warranty work. Also, ask about promised response times and estimated turnaround times.

Tip #18

Figure out your cost of downtime and invest accordingly in spare PC hardware.

✓ **Save on Soft Costs**

✓ **Save on Out-of-Pocket Expenses**

If your small business has more than a handful of PCs, in time you'll develop a service history and learn what kinds of hardware items break fairly regularly.

You'll also see how to convince your PC vendor to supply replacement parts under warranty coverage, as well as how to estimate the time for getting the replacement part to your company and installed into the appropriate PC.

A major cost to consider is employee downtime, as well as time spent by your internal guru chasing down the warranty replacement part, perhaps during an inopportune time.

Value of System Downtime

For a quick, back-of-the-napkin calculation of what system downtime *might* be costing your company, consider:

(A) Projected annual revenue _____

(B) Business days per year _____

(C) Hours in a business day _____

Your hourly cost of system downtime = A / [B x C]

For example, if your company plans to do $4,000,000 in annual sales (A) over 250 business days (B), with 8-hour days (C), your hourly cost of system downtime is $2,000 ($4,000,000 divided by 250 days times 8 hours a day).

Great Spares

***Relative Cost Indicator:* $-$$**

Consider a basic mouse, for example. Most PC vendors would be happy to cover such an inexpensive item under the standard warranty. However, given that you could purchase a spare replacement mouse for about $10 to $30, is it really worth one of your employees being without a mouse, or worse yet without a PC, for a day or two while you await the cross-shipped replacement part under your warranty coverage?

Now your internal guru still may want to pursue getting the broken mouse replaced under warranty coverage. But if you have a spare mouse on hand, at least the warranty claim can be deferred a few days, or a few weeks, until time permits. In the interim, you've mitigated the downtime for a *very* nominal advanced planning expense.

Similarly, keeping a spare keyboard and monitor at your office makes sense. Again, the cost of these items is *very* inexpensive relative to the potential productivity loss while you're waiting for replacement parts to arrive. These three external items also have a unique appeal: They can all be installed rapidly by a PC beginner, without going near the innards of the PC.

Spare Desktop PCs

Relative Cost Indicator: $$-$$$

As the price of entry-level desktop PCs has plummeted and expectations for zero downtime have risen, we've also seen small businesses purchasing an extra PC, to keep fully-configured and ready to plug in on a moment's notice.

In the old days of expensive PC hardware, small businesses used to routinely spend $100 to upgrade their warranty from one year to three years on-site coverage.

But today, if your standard, fully-configured entry-level desktop PC only costs around $600, an office with as few as six PCs can fully fund the purchase of a spare desktop PC, simply by self-insuring on the warranty coverage for years two and three. At the same time, consider how much the $600 desktop PC really is worth on paper (after depreciation) following years one and two.

Again, I'm not advocating that you haul broken desktop PC equipment out to the dumpster. However, I do *strongly* recommend that you invest some of your technology budget in *select* spare parts, and a full desktop PC, so that you can handle warranty claims at *your* leisure, *not* when your company is swamped and functioning in panic mode. And if you're outsourcing this sort of work to a local computer consultant, keeping spares on hand will lessen the need to pay costly emergency rate premiums.

Tip #19

Dispose of PCs properly.

✓ **Save on Soft Costs**

Save on Out-of-Pocket Expenses

Years ago, your company never would've had a problem finding a taker for an old PC. After your small business got four or five productive years out of a system, you may have given it to an employee to take home, or offered employees the opportunity to purchase the retired PC for an *extremely* nominal amount. Alternatively, many donated PCs to local schools, charities or nonprofit organizations.

In the past several years, this has all changed. In the U.S., about 60 percent of households own at least one PC. Schools and charities have become so deluged with PC donations that many get more selective on the equipment they're willing to accept.

In many areas, it's illegal to dispose of a PC in a dumpster. Rather, the PC needs to be recycled. So how do you accomplish this?

Several PC and electronics recycling programs and resources can help you comply with various environmental regulations as you dispose of long obsolete hardware.

- **Dell Asset Recovery Services** -- www.dellfinancialservices.com/solutions/asset_reco very.asp

- **EIA Environment: Consumer Education Initiative (CEI)** -- www.eiae.org

- **Gateway.com: Recycle/Donate Your Old PC** -- www.gateway.com/home/programs/tradein_recycle. shtml

- **HP Environment: Return and Recycling** -- www.hp.com/hpinfo/community/environment/recycl e.htm

- **IBM PC Recycling Service** -- www.ibm.com/ibm/environment/products/pcrservice .phtml

- **International Association of Electronics Recyclers** -- www.iaer.org

- **National Safety Council (U.S.) EPR2 Project Electronic Equipment Recyclers --**
  www.nsc.org/ehc/epr2/cntctlst.htm

Note:

If any of the Web site page addresses above are invalid by the time you're using this list, start at the home page of the Web site and look for any links related to asset management, disposal or recycling. You also can try that Web site's search function or site map to look for recycling information.

Tip #20

If you go the "white-box" route, apply the same support cost-reduction scrutiny.

✓ **Save on Soft Costs**

Save on Out-of-Pocket Expenses

Although this chapter has referred extensively to computer support issues to consider when buying desktop PCs and notebooks from the giant PC vendors, many small businesses purchase "white-box" or "clone" PC products.

"White-Box" PC Market

"White-box" PCs, and servers to a lesser extent, are assembled by local value added resellers (VARs), or network integrators, as opposed to being manufactured in large volumes by global PC giants such as Compaq, Dell and Gateway.

Throughout 1998 and 1999, many industry forecasters, myself included, were predicting the end of the clone PC. After all, between plummeting prices on brand-name PCs and the uncertainty about Year 2000 compliance, the future of unbranded PCs looked murky at best. And hard data bore out this trend.

CRN (www.crn.com, formerly *Computer Reseller News*) has been tracking the "white-box" affinity of computer resellers for several years. Although *CRN* saw a decline in the "white-box" market throughout most of 1999 and into early 2000, there's been a rebound ever since. The market for "cloned" desktop PCs and servers remains remarkably healthy.

Why Resellers Love Selling the "White-Box"

Call them what you will: solution providers, value added resellers, systems or network integrators or technology providers, but many prefer to sell "white-box" PC hardware, as opposed to brand-name PC hardware, for three basic reasons.

First, the solution provider has *complete* control over every hardware component that goes into the system. This not only allows the solution provider to satisfy virtually any small business client whim, but the solution provider can position its custom PC assembly as a master craft, as opposed to a commodity that's manufactured in a factory.

Second, solution providers cite how they are able to respond *immediately* to warranty service needs, as they already have replacement parts in stock.

Finally, solution providers still routinely see 20 to 25 percent net profit margins on "white-box" desktop PCs and servers. Selling comparable brand-name products likely would net *low* single-digit profit margins, if the solution provider breaks even at all.

The third reason obviously helps to ensure the financial survival of solution providers, but small businesses evaluating the pros and cons of brand-name PCs, as opposed to "white-box" PCs, need to evaluate several other factors.

Ask for the Same Deal

Most important, don't let your local "white-box"-selling technology provider off the hook too easily.

Use the preceding 19 points in this chapter to help you decide whether you're doing *everything* in your power to lower your company's PC hardware-specific computer support costs.

The Bottom Line

As PC hardware prices continue to fall, you may be tempted to pay less attention to hardware selection. However, how you choose product lines, vendors, bundled components and soft services can have an *enormous* impact on your small business computer support costs.

Use this chapter as your basis for making more disciplined desktop PC and notebook selections that will yield lower PC support expenses.

Resource Box

- **APC (American Power Conversion)** -- www.apcc.com

- **CNET Shopper** -- www.shopper.com

- **Compaq Computer** -- www.compaq.com

- *CRN* (formerly *Computer Reseller News*) -- www.crn.com

- **Dell Asset Recovery Services** -- www.dellfinancialservices.com/solutions/asset_reco very.asp

- **Dell Computer** -- www.dell.com

- **eBay** -- www.ebay.com

- **EIA Environment: Consumer Education Initiative (CEI)** -- www.eiae.org

- **Gartner Dataquest** -- www.gartner.com

- **Gateway** -- www.gateway.com

- **Gateway.com: Recycle/Donate Your Old PC** -- www.gateway.com/home/programs/tradein_recycle. shtml

- **Hewlett Packard** -- www.hp.com

- **HP Environment: Return and Recycling** -- www.hp.com/hpinfo/community/environment/recycl e.htm

- **IBM** -- www.ibm.com

- **IBM PC Recycling** -- www.ibm.com/environment/

- **IBM PC Recycling Service** -- www.ibm.com/ibm/environment/products/pcrservice.phtml

- **International Association of Electronics Recyclers** -- www.iaer.org

- **Joshua Feinberg's Small Biz Tech Talk** -- www.smallbiztechtalk.com

- **Microsoft** -- www.microsoft.com

- **National Safety Council (U.S.) EPR2 Project Electronic Equipment Recyclers** -- www.nsc.org/ehc/epr2/cntctlst.htm

- **Palm** -- www.palm.com

- *PC Magazine* -- www.pcmag.com

- **TechBargains** -- www.techbargains.com

Free E-mail Newsletter:
Would you like a convenient way to keep up with new tips and techniques from Small Biz Tech Talk? Take control of your technology now! Subscribe to the free bi-weekly Tips newsletter at www.smallbiztechtalk.com

---

Chapter 2
PC Peripherals
Modems, Printers, PDAs and Plug and Play

Choosing the right hardware is a crucial part of planning a cost-effective set of small business computing standards. In Chapter 1, we saw how to jump-start your cost savings by reevaluating how your company purchases desktop PCs and notebooks.

Now, let's shift gears and look at money-saving techniques for modems and printers, two of the most popular, but unfortunately also the most headache-prone, PC peripherals out there in small businesses. Then we'll round out this chapter and Part I with some money-saving tips for scanners, digital cameras, personal digital assistants (PDAs) and Plug and Play.

Tip #21

Select external modems whenever possible.

✓ **Save on Soft Costs**

Save on Out-of-Pocket Expenses

Small businesses often are attracted to the low prices of internal modems. However, this often ends up being the fool's bargain, as you may spend an unusually large amount of time and frustration on configuration and troubleshooting chores related to a nonstandard or difficult-to-install internal modem.

Even though an external modem is almost always more expensive than a generic-brand internal modem, your installation and ongoing support costs are minimized by predictable, easy-to-configure, standardized hardware.

Unless you have some rather unusual circumstances, stick with external modems on your desktop PCs and servers. Here's why.

- **External modems can be reset** without having to reboot your PC.

- **The status indicator lights** on the modem will help you participate more actively in over-the-phone troubleshooting with your ISP's technical support group, for example, or your computer consultant.

- **Because external modems are modular** and outside the PC chassis, external modems are easy to replace during troubleshooting.

Tip:
Most small businesses place external modems on top of their desktop PC system unit or monitor. This is a great location for troubleshooting and resetting the modem, but the modem often falls and easily can break. You can prevent this misfortune by attaching a few short strips of Velcro to both the external modem and PC system unit or monitor.

Tip #22

If you insist on getting internal modems, at least get them factory installed.

✓ **Save on Soft Costs**

Save on Out-of-Pocket Expenses

If you have some irrefutable business or technical reason you absolutely *must* have an internal modem, there are strong, compelling benefits for getting it installed by the PC vendor.

Eliminating Compatibility Guesswork

For starters, your PC vendor will take the compatibility guesswork out of the equation.

This means you'll know that the modem works with your unique PC hardware and operating system combination. This integration work often can save you anywhere from a half-hour to several hours of initial installation frustration.

Ability to Call for Support

Also, your PC vendor *should* consider the internal modem a part of its overall supported solution.

So you should be able to contact the PC vendor's technical support group for a second opinion on troubleshooting the modem, if necessary.

Folded Into System Warranty

Finally, a factory installed internal modem likely would be incorporated into any overall system warranty coverage.

This should provide similar soft cost benefits to those we discussed in Chapter 1, in the context of CD-RW drives and Ethernet network adapters.

Tip #23

Be sure your modems are on the Hardware Compatibility List for your operating system.

✓ **Save on Soft Costs**

Save on Out-of-Pocket Expenses

Modems and Your Version of Microsoft Windows

You can take a lot of the guesswork out of selecting a modem by checking out the Microsoft Windows Hardware Compatibility List (www.microsoft.com/hcl).

This free resource, among other things, lists modem manufacturers, models and various degrees of compatibility and certification across different versions of Microsoft Windows operating systems.

Modems and Your Specific PC Hardware Combination

However, Microsoft's Hardware Compatibility List will *not* tell you about any compatibility problems between a modem and specific PC brands and models.

But, if you have an extremely popular desktop PC model, for example a Dell Dimension or a Compaq Deskpro, some modem vendors will supply this compatibility testing information either on their Web site or through their technical support groups.

Tip:
If you cannot get decent information from a hardware vendor, such as a modem manufacturer, *before* the purchase, run fast, *very* fast to another vendor.

Tip #24

Protect your modems from lightning storms and other dangerous power fluctuations.

✓ **Save on Soft Costs**

✓ **Save on Out-of-Pocket Expenses**

Standard Surge Protectors Are Not Enough

Even if you remember to properly equip your fleet of PCs with various power protection devices such as surge protectors and battery backup units (UPS units), don't forget about your modems.

Just as susceptible to crippling power surges through electricity as through telephone lines, modems need data line protection. This kind of protection shields your PC hardware from power surges and spikes that can enter your PC through your modem and telephone lines.

Avoiding Modem Electrocution with Data Line Protection

Make sure your surge protectors and UPS units *all* include data line protection. The goods news: Even relatively inexpensive surge protectors and UPS units now include data line protection as a standard feature.

Even more important, make sure data line protection is being used properly. Just as a surge protector or UPS unit sits between your PC hardware and an electric outlet, data line protection *must* be placed between your modem and the telephone jack.

Take this recommendation seriously and highlight these paragraphs. I've seen some small businesses get hit with *extremely* heavy hardware damage to both modems and PC systems by ignoring the need for data line protection. Don't become one of these statistics when the prevention is *so* inexpensive and easy to implement.

Note:
Chapter 7 deals with saving money with power protection.

Tip #25

Get more speed and reliability out of your modems with well planned inside telephone wiring.

✓ **Save on Soft Costs**

✓ **Save on Out-of-Pocket Expenses**

Because this chapter is discussing analog modems, you may be wondering whether there's an easy way to get more speed and more reliable performance out of your basic modem and analog telephone line.

56Kbps: Largely Just Marketing Fluff

The 56Kbps description that accompanies analog modems in the USA *always* has a disclaimer. Because of FCC regulations, you'll never get more than 53.3Kbps out of the device.

Note:

Because the V.92 modem standard was *so* new when we went to print, and because there are basically *no* major implementations among leading ISPs yet, most of the information in this next section is based on V.90 modems. V.92 modems should offer faster upload speed, quicker call setup and handshake negotiations, as well as on hold support for Internet call waiting. It remains to be seen whether any of these benefits ever reach mass market.

Can Only Go So Fast Without a Digital Line on Receiving End

The only way you'll ever get anywhere near that 53.3Kbps download speed is by dialing into a modem that has a digital connection (i.e. a T1 line or something similar) to the local telephone company's central office ("CO").

This means, if you have an analog modem on your home computer and you're connecting to an analog modem in your office, you'll never surpass 33.6Kbps connection speeds unless your office has some kind of digital line to the local telephone company's central office.

You generally can connect to your ISP at speeds between 33.6Kbps and 53.3Kbps because your ISP leases digital lines from the local telephone company.

Geography: Beyond Your Control

What else influences your analog connection speed?

The distance between your location and your telephone company's central office is a *major* determinant in your connection speed with an analog modem.

An office that's only 500 feet from the telephone company's central office will, other things being equal, get a much better connection speed than an office that's 5,000 feet or more from the telephone company's central office. Short of relocating your office down the road, there's not much you can do about this.

Note:
Your office's distance to the local telephone company central office is also a major determinant of whether your company qualifies for high-speed DSL-based Internet access.

What You Can Control: Inside Wiring

However, you *do* have some control over conditions once the telephone cabling enters your office -- what's known in the telecommunications industry as inside wiring.

Try to minimize the distance between the location telephone service enters your office and your modem telephone jacks. This point of entry is often referred to as your network interface device (NID) or demarcation point (demarc).

Also, make sure there are no in-line splices or obviously poor cabling conditions between your NID and modem telephone jack.

Finally, make sure the connections on the NID and your modem telephone jack are secure and properly terminated. You often can get an immediate improvement in modem speed by having these connections rechecked and reterminated (known by techies as "punching down" the cable).

Tip:
In many locations, the local telephone company no longer has a monopoly over inside wiring. Regardless of whether your small business has authority over your inside telephone cabling or your landlord takes care of it, most telephone system resellers and electricians now routinely get involved in installing category 5 and category 3 copper cabling. This competition often can mean lower prices and better service. Some small businesses and homeowners now even do a limited amount of their own inside telephone cabling.

Tip #26

Regularly update your modem device drivers and firmware.

✓ **Save on Soft Costs**

Save on Out-of-Pocket Expenses

Just as software applications and operating systems need interim updates between major version upgrades, the software that makes your modem work properly requires updates as well.

About Device Drivers

Modem software generally falls into one of two areas: device drivers and firmware. By updating this software, you often get performance enhancements, new features and bug fixes.

Glossary:
Have you visited this book's Glossary yet? Get a quick refresher on over 160 terms used throughout this book – all those buzzwords and acronyms frequently thrown around by computer consultants and other techies. The Glossary, with extensive cross-references and chapter references, begins on page 231.

A device driver is simply a small piece of software code that allows a modem, or other hardware device, to properly communicate with the operating system and PC hardware. Device drivers for modems, and other devices, almost always are available on diskettes or CD-ROMs that ship with the product.

Note:
Before updating *any* software on your PC, always plan ahead and make appropriate system backups. For details, see Chapter 5, Tip #75: *Prepare a safety net before installing software updates.*

Downloading

You also usually can download the most current device driver from the modem manufacturer's Web site. The Microsoft Windows operating systems also frequently include hundreds of stable, mature device drivers for a variety of modem manufacturers and models.

Since the rise of the Internet and World Wide Web in the mid-'90s, it's gotten a *lot* easier to stay on top of the latest hardware device drivers and firmware updates. Most PC peripheral vendors now have content-rich technical support Web sites with frequently asked questions (FAQs), how-to articles, white papers and software downloads.

Tip:
If you want to be notified automatically of new device drivers and firmware updates, sign up for free e-mail newsletters on vendor Web sites. As you go around to each modem manufacturer's technical support Web site, take note of any available newsletter subscriptions that can help you keep your modems current.

Tip #27

To combat rapid obsolescence, insist on only buying flash-able modems.

✓ **Save on Soft Costs**

✓ **Save on Out-of-Pocket Expenses**

In addition to device drivers, success with modems also largely depends on something called firmware code. Firmware is a piece of software that, instead of being loaded onto your PC's hard drive, gets burned into a chip on the main circuit board of your modem. Just like device drivers, firmware gets updated from time to time. Firmware updates generally are distributed on modem manufacturers' Web sites.

Why Upgrade Firmware?

You often can solve modem compatibility problems or optimize the performance of a modem by upgrading the firmware. At the same time you upgrade modem firmware, also upgrade the device driver software.

Note:
Sometimes device driver versions will work *only* with certain firmware versions. Watch out for this hidden modem configuration trap -- an issue with other PC peripherals as well.

This discussion assumes that your modem has *upgradeable* or flash-able firmware, which helps protect your modem investment and ensures a longer useful life. Upgradeable firmware is often among the features that separate a bargain-basement modem from one that actually will work *reliably* with minimal configuration headaches.

Not as Difficult as it Sounds

Although flashing a modem may sound terribly complex and risky, it generally involves little more than downloading and running a quick software application that reprograms one of the chips on your modem.

Note:
If you own a V.90 modem, you may be able to upgrade to the V.92 standard for free by downloading and flashing the firmware. For details, contact your modem manufacturer or visit its Web site.

Tip #28

Be sure you've got space for the modem you're ordering.

✓ **Save on Soft Costs**

✓ **Save on Out-of-Pocket Expenses**

In the mid-'90s, I was on a brief consulting engagement with a widely known brokerage firm. The purpose of the project was to streamline companywide procurement procedures for *everything* related to desktop PCs, notebooks and servers. Because many managers had generous technology budgets, one of the biggest problems was that new PCs were being ordered with more internal peripherals than the PCs could handle.

The firm's standard desktop PC at the time had three 16-bit ISA expansion slots. The big problem: When a PC was ordered with add-on peripherals that required more than three 16-bit ISA expansion slots, no one was red-flagging the purchase order as potentially troublesome. We couldn't change the company standard desktop PC, so we put together some checklists and internal controls. In a matter of weeks, the procurement problem was history.

Although 16-bit ISA expansion slots are now more of a historical curiosity, make sure your desktop PC, notebook or server has sufficient space for the modem or modems you're planning to purchase. Here's a quick rundown on common modem interfaces and some potential hidden complications.

Note:
Be *extra* sure the modem you're ordering has device drivers for your desired operating system.

Internal Modem

Relative Cost Indicator: $

Depending on the modem type, you'll probably need an available 32-bit PCI expansion slot – or a 16-bit ISA expansion slot if the modem is very dated. If you're purchasing a new PC, check the specs or contact the vendor for clarification. If the modem is for an existing PC, the best way to check this out is simply by removing the case of the computer and looking around.

However, external modems still generally are *much* easier to install and troubleshoot. For details, see Tip #21 earlier in this chapter.

Tip:
Aside from 32-bit performance advantages, a PCI modem makes for *much* easier configuration than a comparable ISA modem, because PCI devices can share certain internal resources called IRQs or interrupts.

External Modem (Serial Based)

Relative Cost Indicator: $-$$

If the modem requires a 9-pin or 25-pin serial port, be sure your PC has one available. Because an increasing number of entry-level desktop PCs only include a single serial port (presumably to keep costs down), make sure you don't have any other devices that need a serial port, such as a digital camera, serial printer or UPS.

Tip:
If you run into a bona fide serial-port shortage, you always can purchase an aftermarket expansion card that will give you one or more additional serial ports. I've used products from both Digi (www.digi.com) and SIIG (www.siig.com).

External Modem (USB Based)

Relative Cost Indicator: $-$$

If you choose a newer external modem that uses a USB port, as opposed to a serial port, be sure your desired operating system supports USB *and* that your PC has an available USB port -- or that you purchase an appropriate USB expansion hub.

Note:
USB stands for Universal Serial Bus and was generally *not* supported under Microsoft Windows NT Workstation 4 (and earlier), as well as early versions of Microsoft Windows 95.

PCMCIA, PC Card or CardBus (32) Modem for Notebooks

Relative Cost Indicator: $$

Although there are ways to extend the use of credit card-sized expansion cards to desktop PCs and servers, this kind of modem largely is used for notebooks. In this scenario, make sure you have one or more available PCMCIA Type II slots for the modem.

Many major notebook manufacturers now include built-in 56Kbps modems and 10/100Mbps Ethernet network adapters. These are *great* features to get bundled into a notebook purchase.

First, the implied price is usually an *excellent* value.

Plus you get *tons* of soft cost benefits, such as the kind we explored in Chapter 1 in the context of bundled components.

Finally, your PCMCIA slots remain freed up for future expansion, such as adding wireless networking capabilities.

Tip:

If you want to use a PCMCIA modem or network card without a dongle or pigtail cable, which I highly recommend, be sure to evaluate your network card and modem needs at the same time. For instance, Intel's Xircom Real Port product line eliminates the need to worry about broken or lost dongle cables. However, because the Real Port adapter takes up both PCMCIA Type II slots in a typical notebook, you'll likely want to purchase one of Intel's Xircom combo cards to cover both LAN and modem connectivity needs.

Tip #29

Know your options for getting up to date printer device drivers.

✓ **Save on Soft Costs**

Save on Out-of-Pocket Expenses

Just as with modems, there are often different versions of printer device drivers that affect your computer support efforts.

Microsoft-Supplied Printer Drivers

If you want the most stable printer driver, albeit sometimes not the most current, Microsoft-supplied drivers are generally your best bet.

The Microsoft Windows operating systems include hundreds of drivers for the most popular printers.

Drivers That Ship With the Printer

However, nearly all printers include a CD-ROM, from the printer manufacturer, that contains printer drivers and any related utility software.

Because printer manufacturers frequently include related accessory programs and utilities to help you get the most out of the printer, you might feel shortchanged if you rely solely on the Microsoft-supplied printer drivers.

But if all you need are the limited capabilities of the printer, or if you want to run an older emulation mode on the printer, the Microsoft tested OS-bundled driver may be the better choice.

Downloadable Printer Drivers

As a third option, most printer manufacturers distribute updated printer drivers and utility programs on their Web sites.

This resource becomes particularly relevant if you purchase a discontinued printer that may have been sitting on the store shelf or in a warehouse for six months or more.

By visiting the printer manufacturer's Web site, you may able to download a more current device driver for your printer.

Tip #30

Prepare a road warrior printer driver survival kit for your notebook.

✓ **Save on Soft Costs**

Save on Out-of-Pocket Expenses

Have you ever gotten stuck on the road with your notebook, a sales proposal that needs to get printed out, and access to a printer in a client's office or a hotel business center, *but* you just couldn't seem to print to the available printer? Alas, there's a secret.

Think Lowest-Common-Denominator

Most printers are generally backward compatible. So if you ever need to troubleshoot a popular printer, or don't have access to installation media from the printer vendor or Microsoft, you often can run an older printer driver on a newer printer.

Value of the HP LaserJet Series II Printer Driver

Let's say I'm traveling with my notebook. The hotel business center has a Hewlett Packard LaserJet 5. Even though I don't have that exact device driver installed on my notebook, I keep a Hewlett Packard LaserJet Series II device driver installed for these kinds of situations.

Although I cannot use advanced features of the LaserJet 5 with the LaserJet Series II driver, I *am* able to print out my report just minutes before a client presentation.

Value of the HP DeskJet 500C Printer Driver

The same idea tends to apply to Hewlett Packard DeskJet printers as well. So, what if I'm visiting a client for a day that only has a DeskJet 820Cse? I'd like to print out some revised proposal documents to leave with my client to cinch a crucial deal.

Because I have an older DeskJet 500C printer driver on my notebook's hard drive, I'm able to print out the document on the DeskJet 820Cse and close the sale on the spot.

Note:
Starting with Microsoft Windows 2000, Microsoft includes a device driver cache folder to prevent getting stuck on the road driver-less.

Tip #31

Pay attention to your printer's cost per page.

Save on Soft Costs

✓ **Save on Out-of-Pocket Expenses**

Small businesses often gravitate toward low-cost inkjet and entry-level laser printers. Given the *extremely* reasonable price tags (in the neighborhood of $100 to $400) this *seems* to make sense at first. But this cost-savings strategy often falls apart on closer scrutiny and seems myopic in retrospect.

Inkjet Cost Fallacy

Inkjet printers, although *very* inexpensive to purchase, often have an *extraordinarily* high cost per page for cartridge supplies. It's not uncommon for inkjet cost per page analyses to work out to $0.08 for black ink, with *very* moderate page coverage, and $0.25 for color ink, again with moderate page coverage.

So, for a relatively low volume, say a ream or two of paper each month, the supply costs don't get too painful. But, crank up the volume a few notches to a case or two of paper each month, and you will *pay through the nose* for supplies.

But what if you really need *some* color? You're still better off using a black-and-white laser printer for your regular correspondence, and sparingly leveraging an inkjet printer for occasional color printing needs.

Laser Printer Supply Cost Differences

An entry-level black-and-white laser printer, in the $300 to $600 price range, typically has cost per page expenses around $0.04 to $0.05. Although this is still *substantially* less expensive than operating an inkjet printer for a moderate volume, entry-level laser printers still don't make sense for many paper-intensive small businesses.

Entry-level laser printers have a *much* higher cost per page than workgroup laser printers. In addition, entry-level laser printers have *much* lighter duty cycles -- the monthly volume threshold after which your laser printer is likely to wave a white flag and surrender.

Tip #32

If your monthly volume merits, invest in a networked workgroup laser printer to drive down your support costs and cost per page.

✓ **Save on Soft Costs**

✓ **Save on Out-of-Pocket Expenses**

Investing in a workgroup laser printer is often the best bet for a small business. Depending on the manufacturer, product, networking capabilities and advanced paper handling features, workgroup laser printers typically cost anywhere from $900 to $1,500 (and up).

Tip:
In larger companies, shared network printers are the de facto standard. Only users dealing with *highly* sensitive data typically get their own personal printer.

Lowest Cost Per Page and Most Durability

With a workgroup laser printer, you'll generally see a cost per page of around $0.025 to $0.03.

You'll also have *no* problem handling high printing volumes, on the order of several cases of paper each month.

Double Duty as a Photocopy Machine

For very small offices, a workgroup laser printer with a printing speed of 25 pages a minute or more often can serve double duty as a photocopy machine replacement, if most or all of your documents already are digitized, or if you keep a flatbed scanner with the copy machine function near the printer.

Cost Comparisons: Inkjet, Personal Laser Printer and Workgroup Laser Printer

Let's say you're outfitting a small office with six PC users and planning to install a LAN. What makes the most sense?

A) **Six inkjet printers**, around $200 each ($1,200 total)

B) **Six entry-level laser printers**, around $400 each
($2,400 total)

C) **One high-speed networked workgroup laser
printer**, around $1,500. *And* for occasional color print-
ing, one inkjet printer (around $200), shared on a peer-
to-peer basis ($1,700 total)

Unless you have some out of the ordinary requirements, I'd almost
always recommend option C. The bigger challenge is convincing the six
users to give up their personal printers.

Organizational and Behavioral Barriers

All of a sudden you're asking employees to walk a few feet to pick
up printouts when they were used to the convenience of their own
printers on their desks.

If you *really* are committed to keeping your costs as low as possible,
and getting your office a more reliable, high-volume printer, your employees simply may have to learn to share.

A Colorful Future

If you have a high-volume color printing requirement, you once
only had two choices: swallow hard and pay sky-high prices for inkjet
printer cartridges, or outsource the color printing to a local service bu-
reau.

Now that brand-name, color laser printers have dropped below
$2,000, many small businesses will purchase color laser printers rap-
idly to drive down their cost per page, while producing *much* crisper
and more professional-looking color printouts.

Tip #33

Get more pages out of your laser printer toner cartridges.

Save on Soft Costs

✓ **Save on Out-of-Pocket Expenses**

Although this next money-saving tip has been around for a long time, I'm always surprised by how few small businesses actually use it.

The End is Not Necessarily *The* End

Just as an inkjet printer cartridge does, laser printer toner cartridges have a finite life. You'll know you're getting to the end of the toner cartridge's capacity when your pages start to get streaks and the printing appears lighter.

At that point, there's still usually plenty of toner left in the cartridge. It simply needs to be redistributed.

Toner Conserved = Money Saved on Supply Costs

To do so, remove the toner cartridge from the printer and shake it a few times, in much the same way you shake the cartridge before installing it into the printer.

Amazingly enough, the first time you do this, shaking the toner cartridge generally will buy you a few hundred extra pages. For argument's sake, let's value that around $8 to $10.

Sooner or later, you'll start to see the same characteristic streaks. Once again, you can remove the toner cartridge; shake it up a few times, then reinsert.

You'll find that, each time you repeat the shaking exercise, you'll get fewer and fewer pages out of the toner cartridge. Once you've removed, shaken and reinserted three or four times, you've probably squeezed as much life out of the toner cartridge as you possibly can. Then it's time to actually replace it.

And you can glow in the satisfaction of knowing that you were able to extend the life of your toner cartridge by at least 10 to 15 percent. In a typical office, this kind of savings *really* can add up in a year or less.

Tip #34

Troubleshoot your printer as the pros do.

✓ **Save on Soft Costs**

Save on Out-of-Pocket Expenses

When your inkjet or laser printer starts acting a little unusual, there's one very simple thing you can try *before* placing a call for on-site service or technical support. It's called a printer self-test, and nearly every printer has one built in.

Know the Self-Test Drill for Your Printers

Now, the trick is that each printer model has a *slightly* different way of activating the self-test mode. So dig out the booklet that came with the printer and find out how your printer does its self-test. Or you probably can find this information on the printer manufacturer's technical support Web site.

Note:
The self-test I'm referring to here is built into the printer firmware (i.e. a hardware-based test). This shouldn't be confused with a Print Test Page you can generate from Microsoft Windows by viewing your printer properties. If you're trying to go up the troubleshooting ladder in a logical fashion, a hardware-based self-test *always* should precede a Microsoft Windows software-based Print Test Page effort.

On many inkjet printers, you can generate a self-test page if you hold down a button while you turn the printer on. On many laser printers, you find the self-test mode by scrolling through some of the functions on the LCD menu.

Ruling Out Variables: Methodical Troubleshooting

Regardless of how you reach the built in diagnostics, the internal printer self-test runs *independently* of your PC. In fact, you *should* unplug the parallel printer, serial or network cable while running an internal self-test.

The self-test should generate one or more status pages that tell you all the vital stats you'd ever want to know about your printer.

Tip:
Run a self-test while your printer is healthy so you have a baseline for comparison when something starts acting up.

A self-test also will help you rule out variables and concentrate your troubleshooting on the most relevant areas. For example, if the self-test reveals you have some kind of *very* fundamental mechanical failure with the printer, don't bother trying to troubleshoot your printing from Microsoft Word or a similar software program.

Companion CD-ROM

Are you ready to take your cost-savings to the next level, but you're at a loss for the *right* questions to ask? Check out the Companion CD-ROM for *What Your Computer Consultant Doesn't Want You to Know* -- with over 550 Action Items to get you started saving money right now.

The Action Items are presented in a variety of convenient file formats including Adobe Acrobat .pdf, HTML, Microsoft Word .doc and Microsoft Excel .xls. In addition, the Action Items are loaded up in a Microsoft Outlook Personal Folders File (.pst) -- ready for you to import into your Microsoft Outlook Tasks. The Companion CD-ROM also includes an electronic Resource Directory, recapping the book's suggested Web sites, that's all set for you to import into your Microsoft Internet Explorer Favorites list. Use the handy Action Item format to copy, paste and delegate -- while you tailor the money-saving program to your company's unique needs.

For more information on the Companion CD-ROM, see page 285.

Or visit www.smallbiztechtalk.com/tools/ to download sample Action Items or order the Companion CD-ROM.

Tip #35

Proceed carefully to avoid making printer jams worse.

✓ **Save on Soft Costs**

Save on Out-of-Pocket Expenses

A printer jam needn't be so catastrophic as it first seems. However, the way you go about trying to clear the paper jam can make all the difference in the world between success and needing an expensive repair.

Avoid Rushing

The big secret in clearing paper jams always centers around removing the *entire* obstruction as a single piece. You may be tempted to grab at whatever corners you possibly can reach, figuring that you'll get the rest of the obstruction on subsequent passes. However, this can be a sure ticket to failure.

The problem is, once the obstruction breaks up into smaller pieces, you're bound to leave a few slivers behind, no matter how careful you are. So how can you maximize your chances of success in removing the entire obstruction at once?

Five Steps for Clearing Jams

1) **Remove any remaining paper**, envelopes or sheets of labels from your intake and trays.

2) **Remove paper tray(s)** -- Next, if the printer has a removable cassette or tray that holds the intake paper, remove that tray so you can get a better view of any clogged areas of the printer.

3) **Get a view of the toner/ink area** -- Then open the area where the inkjet or toner cartridge meets the paper and, if you can, remove the inkjet or toner cartridge to give yourself better access to the obstruction.

4) **Open up the rear door** -- Finally, if your printer has a back door for a straight paper path, open the rear tray. Once again inspect for any less obvious obstructions.

5) **Now start pulling evenly** -- *After* you've thoroughly surveyed the paper path, from start to finish, begin pulling *gently* on the obstruction and applying force at different places evenly, until you're able to remove the *entire* obstruction at once.

Tip #36

Know the risks of using refilled and remanufactured inkjet and toner cartridges.

✓ **Save on Soft Costs**

✓ **Save on Out-of-Pocket Expenses**

Many small business owners swear by the cost-saving concept of purchasing refilled and remanufactured inkjet and toner cartridges, but I am not among them.

Knock Off Supplies Are Not Cheap

Since dot matrix printers became as extinct as the dodo bird in the early '90s, I've owned several inkjet and laser printers. Although I sometimes wish the printer manufacturers' supply prices were lower, I've never regretted paying for quality printer supplies.

Of course, I actively seek out any sales, promotions or rebates on genuine printer consumables. But, as a technology professional, I just don't consider the cost savings of knock off printer supplies to be worth the risk.

Minimizing Repair Costs

In all my years, I've *never* had a messy inkjet or toner spill. I've also hardly ever needed to repair printers, and the printers I've purchased generally have become obsolete before a repair was needed.

So, ultimately, I've kept my printer support costs exceptionally low. I know there are other care and feeding factors to consider, but I attribute a major portion of this success to sticking with the recommended printer supplies.

And because the included manufacturer's printer warranty generally covers only a fraction of its useful life, I've had (and continue to have) *every* incentive in the world to ensure that my printers don't need to have expensive, out-of-warranty repairs.

Tip #37

Analyze the pros and cons of out-of-warranty printer repairs.

Save on Soft Costs

✓ **Save on Out-of-Pocket Expenses**

As with other aging hardware assets, many times it doesn't pay to spend money on an out-of-warranty printer repair.

Estimating the Value of an Aging Printer

Before agreeing to an expensive, out-of-warranty printer repair, always factor in the age of the printer, how it stacks up against newer models on the market and the replacement cost of the device.

For example, if my Hewlett Packard LaserJet 5 were to need a major repair, I'd have to investigate whether the repair would be a worthwhile investment. In 1997, the LaserJet 5 cost around $1,000. So I *definitely* got lots of good years and volume out of the device. Moreover, for around the same price I paid, I can get a new replacement laser printer, with a one-year warranty, that's a minimum of two to three times faster than my existing printer.

Cost of a Repair vs. Putting That Money Toward Replacement

So if I could repair my LaserJet 5 for $100 to $200, I'd probably make the investment and consider it a good spare printer for the future. If the cost were considerably more, I'd probably opt to purchase the newer model.

With most *in*expensive inkjet printers, it almost *never* pays to spend money on an out-of-warranty repair. The replacement cost of a new printer is just *too* low, relative to the minimum cost of a service call. To put this all in perspective, think about an out-of-warranty inkjet printer repair the same way you'd look at the prospect of repairing an inexpensive, outdated TV or VCR.

Tip #38

Protect your printers from utility-induced electrical hazards.

✓ **Save on Soft Costs**

✓ **Save on Out-of-Pocket Expenses**

Just like PCs and modems, your printers can get zapped or fried by power spikes and surges. You need to know how to properly guard against these risks.

Real Surge Protectors = Lifesavers

First, install business-grade surge protectors on *all* your printers. Don't be fooled by power strips masquerading as surge protectors. Never plug a printer directly into an electrical outlet. There should always be a surge protector between the printer and the electrical outlet.

Avoiding Battery Backup Units

Just as crucial, don't plug high-volume laser printers into battery backup units. If a power outage causes a paper jam, it won't have anywhere near the impact on your small business as an unprotected desktop PC or server. Be sure to spend your battery backup (UPS) budget to properly protect what needs it most.

Even more relevant, high-volume laser printers generally draw as many amps as small photocopy machines or refrigerators. Thus, their power consumption will monopolize and overload small battery backup units – ultimately depriving the desktop PC or server of crucial battery backup resources.

So the general rule for printers: *Always* provide surge protection, but don't worry about battery backup protection.

Note:
For more power protection tips to save you money, see Chapter 7.

Tip #39

Upgrade laser printer RAM to get a performance boost for a very nominal expense.

✓ **Save on Soft Costs**

✓ **Save on Out-of-Pocket Expenses**

Until very recently, small businesses only added RAM to laser printers if they had relatively unusual or graphics-intensive applications, or were frequently getting memory overload errors. Because laser printer RAM upgrades were rather expensive, it was a rarely recommended upgrade.

Extending the Useful Life of Marginal Laser Printers

However, during 2001, RAM prices fell dramatically.

Even if your laser printer came reasonably well-equipped with RAM and you only have light graphical demands, you can get a substantial performance boost out of your laser printer through an inexpensive memory upgrade.

This also may help you extend the life of a marginal laser printer by a year or more.

Savvy Shopping Tips

You'll probably want to start your RAM upgrade research by visiting your printer manufacturer's Web site, but there's no reason you should feel limited to purchasing the memory upgrade from your printer manufacturer.

There are some very reputable third-party vendors of laser printer RAM upgrades, and most guarantee compatibility.

Tip:

As a starting point, check out Crucial Technology (www.crucial.com) and Kingston Technology (www.kingston.com).

Tip #40

To avoid support headaches, carefully scrutinize the purchase of a flatbed scanner or digital camera.

✓ **Save on Soft Costs**

✓ **Save on Out-of-Pocket Expenses**

Flatbed scanners and digital cameras, insofar as peripheral devices go, have much in common with external modems.

Same Due Diligence Procedure as Modems

As a result, you can use many of the same due diligence techniques for researching these purchases as you did for modems.

Interface and Operating System Issues

Always consider the interface as well as published operating system compatibility lists.

Unbiased Opinions

In addition, look for any independent reviews from trade magazines or Web sites.

Included Goodies

Also, don't forget to ask about bundled software and vendor technical support.

Tip #41

Consider how to cost-effectively support personal digital assistants (PDAs).

✓ **Save on Soft Costs**

Save on Out-of-Pocket Expenses

In the past few years, we have seen a tremendous proliferation of handheld devices, primarily those based on the Palm OS and Microsoft Windows CE Pocket PC design.

The Whole World in Your Hand

In many cases, your internal guru or computer consultant gets the first support request, even when an employee purchased the handheld device on his or her own or received it as a gift.

Inevitably, regardless of whether your small business purchases them for employees, personal digital assistants (PDAs) sooner or later will make their way onto your company's computer support radar screen.

With all the different product and operating system variables to consider, how will your company cost-effectively support PDAs?

There are two main issues to think about: data security and desktop connectivity.

Resource Directory:
Want an easy way to recall the over 60 Web site references discussed in this book? Check out the Resource Directory, starting on page 261, for suggested Web sites that deal with PC hardware and peripherals, software applications and operating systems, data protection and other general small business technology information.

Data Security

Because some PDAs have the ability to remotely connect to your office's LAN, you need to consider PDA remote access, just as you would any other remote device, such as an employee's home computer or a company-owned notebook.

This also should include a thorough discussion of what sensitive data can be stored on a PDA, given that the pocket-sized PDA devices are inherently vulnerable to theft.

In the same context of data security, be sure to establish some kind of backup procedures. We've all heard the horror stories of users losing three years of appointments and 2,000 customer names that were stored on their PDA and not backed up anywhere else. Don't let your small business become one of these statistics.

Desktop Connectivity

Second, think about how your internal guru or computer consultant will assist users in connecting their PDAs to their office PCs.

Yes, your company *could* adopt a policy banning PDAs from the office entirely, or making users responsible for their own PDA-related support issues, but these extreme approaches may *not* be practical.

After all, PDAs are becoming a major competitive force that others in your industry may be rushing to integrate into their information technology toolkit.

In addition, you probably don't want to leave employees to install and support their own PDA desktop connectivity, *unless* they are *very* PC savvy.

All too often, a user inadvertently will break a multitude of key software configurations while accepting default installation settings.

If your company is determined to have users tap the power and flexibility of PDAs, you'll need *someone* PC savvy managing these installations.

Free E-mail Newsletter:
Would you like a convenient way to keep up with new tips and techniques from Small Biz Tech Talk? Take control of your technology now! Subscribe to the free bi-weekly Tips newsletter at www.smallbiztechtalk.com

---

Tip #42

Don't put blind faith in Plug and Play – it doesn't always work as advertised.

✓ **Save on Soft Costs**

✓ **Save on Out-of-Pocket Expenses**

No chapter on money-saving techniques for PC hardware peripherals would be complete without a brief discussion of Plug and Play.

First introduced with Microsoft Windows 95, and gradually revised in successive releases of Microsoft Windows, Plug and Play is *supposed* to provide the ultimate in configuration convenience. When it works, Plug and Play frees you up from most installation and resource assignment chores, which are handled automatically by the operating system.

Nothing Is as Great as It Sounds on the Surface

However, Plug and Play *doesn't always work*. After all, hardware vendors are writing their device drivers and installation routines to support several different versions of Microsoft Windows and millions of possible PC hardware configurations. When Plug and Play doesn't function as expected, it can be a *major* headache to get working properly.

When Plug and Play works, it truly can be a beautiful thing, saving you countless hours of initial installation and configuration frustration. But when it doesn't, you'll know why it's rightly earned the less desirable, satirical nickname of plug and pray.

Doing Your Homework

Often the best way to avoid these configuration hassles is to check thoroughly for operating system and hardware testing results on the vendor's Web site; examine posted results on the Microsoft Windows Hardware Compatibility List (HCL); and most importantly, visit Web sites that conduct independent product reviews.

The Bottom Line

Modems and printers are *very* popular and important peripheral devices for most small businesses. However, both can cause seemingly endless installation, configuration and ongoing support headaches.

If not carefully planned, both modems and printers can rapidly consume a big chunk of your overall technology budget.

In this chapter, we surveyed a variety of easy to apply modem and printer cost-saving techniques you can put to work right away. In addition, we looked at some related cost-control techniques you can apply to other common peripherals and handheld devices.

Resource Box

- **Crucial Technology** -- www.crucial.com

- **Digi** -- www.digi.com

- **Hewlett Packard** -- www.hp.com

- **Joshua Feinberg's Small Biz Tech Talk** -- www.smallbiztechtalk.com

- **Kingston Technology** -- www.kingston.com

- **Microsoft Windows Hardware Compatibility List (HCL)** -- www.microsoft.com/hcl/

- **SIIG** -- www.siig.com

- **Xircom (Intel)** -- www.xircom.com

Table of Tips:
Need a quick refresher on the 101 money-saving tips discussed in this book? Check out the Table of Tips, beginning on page 267, for a chapter-by-chapter recap and quick reference.

Part II

Software Cost-Saving Tips

Chapter 3
Microsoft Office
on the Desktop

Integration, Navigation, Templates, Organization,
Proactive Maintenance and Troubleshooting

In Chapter 2, we looked at several ways to keep your computer support costs under control when dealing with common PC peripherals such as modems and printers. Now, let's examine some simple ways to control your computing expenses with Microsoft Office software applications. Table 3-1 and Table 3-2 show which Microsoft Office family applications are included with each edition of Microsoft Office 2000 and Microsoft Office XP, respectively.

Microsoft Office 2000 Suite Components

	Standard	Small Business	Professional	Premium
Microsoft Word 2000	X	X	X	X
Microsoft Excel 2000	X	X	X	X
Microsoft Outlook 2000	X	X	X	X
Microsoft Publisher 2000		X	X	X
Microsoft Small Business Tools		X	X	X
Microsoft Access 2000			X	X
Microsoft PowerPoint 2000	X		X	X
Microsoft FrontPage 2000				X
Microsoft PhotoDraw 2000				X
Relative Cost Indicator	$	$	$$	$$$

Table 3-1

Avoid expensive ordering mistakes. Know which Microsoft Office programs are included with various editions of Microsoft Office 2000 products. Source: Small Biz Tech Talk.

Microsoft Office XP Suite Components

	Standard	Small Business	Professional	Developer
Microsoft Word 2002	X	X	X	X
Microsoft Excel 2002	X	X	X	X
Microsoft Outlook 2002	X	X	X	X
Microsoft Publisher 2002		X		
Microsoft Access 2002			X	X
Microsoft PowerPoint 2002	X		X	X
Microsoft FrontPage 2002				X
SharePoint Team Services				X
Developer Tools				X
Relative Cost Indicator	$	$	$$	$$$

Table 3-2

There are several different editions of Microsoft Office XP to contend with. Save time and money by purchasing the right one for your needs at the outset. Source: Small Biz Tech Talk.

Note:

Microsoft Office XP Small Business Edition is available *only* when bundled with the purchase of a new PC.

Free E-mail Newsletter:

Would you like a convenient way to keep up with new tips and techniques from Small Biz Tech Talk? Take control of your technology now! Subscribe to the free bi-weekly Tips newsletter at www.smallbiztechtalk.com

Tip #43

Be sure to use the right Microsoft Office application for the job.

✓ **Save on Soft Costs**

✓ **Save on Out-of-Pocket Expenses**

As Microsoft Office applications have become more powerful, through about a half-dozen version upgrades, the line often has become blurred among the numerous software programs.

Avoid Time-Consuming Rookie Mistakes

Don't make the common mistake of using the wrong program for the job (Table 3-3).

Although you can compile a database on a *very* small scale in Microsoft Excel, it's *not* a database management program. Microsoft Access is a *much* better choice.

Although you can prepare desktop publishing documents in Microsoft Word or Microsoft PowerPoint, neither one is a true desktop publishing package. Microsoft Publisher is a *much* better small business choice for most basic desktop publishing needs.

Note:
Although we typeset this book in Microsoft Word, I don't recommend doing so *unless* you are a *strong* intermediate to advanced Microsoft Word user. For garden variety newsletters, brochures, catalogs, flyers and stationery, Microsoft Publisher works *very* well.

We often see small business end users preparing financial statements, or other similar tables, in Microsoft Word. Microsoft Excel is a *much* better choice for anything related to scientific, financial, economic or accounting data. Microsoft Excel also provides plenty of formatting tools to enrich the presentation of this sort of data.

Many times, small businesses will start a simple mailing list database in Microsoft Excel or Microsoft Outlook. However, as the number of fields begins to grow and the volume of records scales up, Microsoft Access becomes a *far* superior choice, for it allows you to manage the mailing list as a relational database.

Commonly Misused Microsoft Office Applications

Task	Misused Application(s)	Better Choice for Most Small Businesses
Contact Management System	Microsoft Excel Microsoft Outlook	Microsoft Access
Desktop Publishing	Microsoft PowerPoint Microsoft Word	Microsoft Publisher
Tables	Microsoft Word	Microsoft Excel

Table 3-3

Although special circumstances may dictate otherwise, many Microsoft Office applications that allow you to start a certain task aren't necessarily the best places to continue performing that task repeatedly – as your company's needs evolve.

Protecting Yourself From Having to Start Over

Fortunately, Microsoft Office applications contain several import and export wizards that guide you through migrating data from one program format to another.

So, for example, if you've built a simple contacts database in Microsoft Excel or Microsoft Outlook, you generally can import the data quite easily into a Microsoft Access database table.

For more detailed information on the features, capabilities and limitations of individual Microsoft Office applications, check out www.microsoft.com/office/

Tip #44

Use Microsoft Office integration to put an end to busy work.

✓ **Save on Soft Costs**

Save on Out-of-Pocket Expenses

A decade ago, it was *very* difficult to complete a mail merge between applications from different vendors' software packages. Don't miss out on one of the most compelling benefits of Microsoft's stronghold over desktop office automation software. Be sure to take advantage of the tight integration across Microsoft products.

Don't Retype It. Merge It!

What are some easy ways you can begin putting this integration to use? Two examples immediately come to mind: mail merge and financial statement tables. Do you need to create automatically, some customized mailing labels, envelopes or form letters, but often end up settling for some low-tech, tedious, scissors-and-glue approach?

The Mail Merge Helper wizard in Microsoft Word makes it *very* easy to pull in address lists, or similar data, from such programs as Microsoft Excel, Microsoft Outlook and Microsoft Access. Don't even think about having your clerical staff retype the information!

Preparing Tables: Just Say No to Spaces and Tabs

Another small business redundancy has to do with preparing financial statements within documents. In most companies, a CFO, accounting manger or controller prepares various financial statements in Microsoft Excel, then passes the information over to an executive assistant to incorporate into regulatory documents, lender and investor updates, and annual reports.

Make sure your company isn't falling into this *huge* productivity trap. Be sure your executive assistant, or whomever is charged with pulling together these documents in Microsoft Word, is aware of simple, *enormous* timesaving shortcuts such as the Paste Special command on the Edit menu (Figure 3-1) and the Object command on the Insert menu (Figure 3-2). All too often, we see the executive assistant *retyping* these financial statements from scratch in Microsoft Word, either by using the Insert Table feature or, even worse, by aligning text by using tabs and spaces. Ouch!

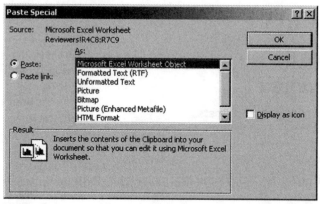

Figure 3-1

Use the Edit, Paste Special command in Microsoft Word to copy and paste a formatted Microsoft Excel worksheet range into your document.

Be Diplomatic and Tread Gently at First

Not all companies will suffer from these same redundancies. But *someone* needs to take the time to go on a fact-finding mission in your organization to spot and remedy at least *some* of these inefficiencies.

Because of the sensitive nature of this, you may be better off leaning on your accountants or auditors for this task. In other cases, there's no reason a PC savvy office manager, controller or CFO can't preclude or successfully manage this exploratory work.

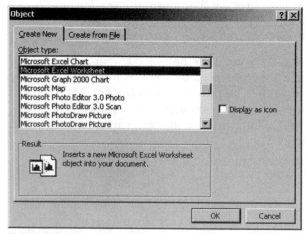

Figure 3-2

Alternatively, use the Insert, Object command in Microsoft Word to easily insert a complete Microsoft Excel worksheet into your document.

Tip #45

Avoid ordering off the menu, if possible.

✓ **Save on Soft Costs**

Save on Out-of-Pocket Expenses

Toolbars in software applications give you point and click access to the most common functions in a particular program. Without toolbar buttons, you'd still be able to get the job done through menus, but you'd end up doing a *lot* more work than you needed to.

Toolbars Rule!

The Toolbars in Microsoft Office applications save time, mouse clicks and keystrokes. Yet, I'm always shocked how many small business PC users are missing out on this *huge* productivity booster. In fact, *not* using Toolbars can be a *major* barrier standing in your way of using Microsoft Word and Microsoft Excel more productively. Most of what you're about to learn also applies to other Microsoft Office applications, including Microsoft Outlook and Microsoft Publisher.

Pull-Down Menus: More Time Consuming

Menus include virtually *every* available command, but you are probably visiting menus a lot more than you need to. For most of us, the great majority of what's needed is in the Standard and the Formatting Toolbars. Table 3-4 lists popular toolbar buttons.

You'll notice a few repeats in Table 3-4, such as Format Painter and Undo/Redo. Again, one of the big benefits of using multiple applications in Microsoft Office is the idea of learn once, apply many places. As you're gaining proficiency in one application, you're already learning small pieces of *all* the other Microsoft Office programs and toolbars.

ScreenTips: What Does That Button Do Again?

Microsoft helps you to easily and quickly recall the function of each Toolbar button with something called ScreenTips. To use the ScreenTip for a particular Toolbar button, simply move your mouse pointer on top of the Toolbar button and leave it hovering there *without* clicking the mouse button.

Toolbar buttons save you *lots* of time in Microsoft Office

Word	Excel
Borders	AutoSum
Columns	Chart Wizard
Format Painter	Drawing
Increase/Decrease Indent	Fill Color
Insert Table	Format Painter
Numbering/Bullets	Merge and Center
Show/Hide	Paste Function
Style	Spelling
Undo/Redo	Sort Ascending/Descending
Zoom	Undo/Redo

Table 3-4

Common buttons on the Standard and Formatting Toolbars in Microsoft Word and Microsoft Excel.

Within a moment, a little yellow box pops up to give you a *very* concise explanation of the Toolbar button's functionality. For example, if I hover on top of the little yellow file folder button on the Standard toolbar in Microsoft Word or Microsoft Excel, a ScreenTip called Open pops up to remind me that this button is used to open a file.

Customizing your Microsoft Office Toolbars

If there are a few missing wish list buttons that still have you trekking to the pull-down menus, you *easily* can customize Toolbars in Microsoft Office applications *without* any programming or even anything remotely technical. Just make a note of the menu command you want on your Toolbar.

Next, go to the Tools menu, Customize command, click on the Commands tab, and find the desired command and icon. Then, drag and drop the command icon up to the appropriate Toolbar with your mouse and release. Voila! If you want to save great amounts of time and make your employees more productive, invest a few minutes and place your most commonly used Microsoft Office commands on various Toolbars.

Tip #46

Learn how to recover a lost toolbar.

✓ **Save on Soft Costs**

Save on Out-of-Pocket Expenses

Toolbar Dependence Syndrome

Once a new Microsoft Office user gets comfortable with Toolbar buttons, the user is likely to virtually abandon use of more complex menu commands. So, panic can rapidly set in a when one of the Toolbars vanishes without a trace. This is one of *the* most common tech support and training requests I see with Microsoft Office users.

Easily Remedied with a Few Minutes of Training

Include some simple training in your employee computer orientation to show how to get back a Toolbar that may have wandered off the screen. You control which Toolbars are displayed through the View menu, Toolbars command. By default, Microsoft Word and Microsoft Excel display the Standard and Formatting Toolbars. You can turn the display of various Toolbars on and off by toggling displayed checkmarks (Figure 3-3).

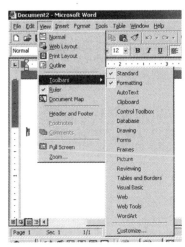

Figure 3-3

Learn how to recover a lost Microsoft Office Toolbar.

Tip #47

Build a Microsoft Word template library to slash your offset printing bills.

✓ **Save on Soft Costs**

✓ **Save on Out-of-Pocket Expenses**

Are you still paying outside companies to print small quantities of envelopes, letterhead, memo pads, vacation request forms, employment applications, employee annual evaluations and potentially *dozens* of other office forms and stationery?

Eliminating Some Outside Printing Costs

Although some unusual circumstances still may justify these old-fashioned practices, most small businesses can save a bundle by setting up various templates in Microsoft Word to eliminate some of your outside printing costs.

Note:
To those of you in the offset printing industry, please understand that I don't have any deep-seated resentment of how you make a living. I'm only the messenger here. On the flip side, however, you're probably in a *fabulous* position to leverage your loyal customer list and graphic design skills to diversify your services and build quite a formidable Web site design business.

Four-Step Plan of Attack

1) **Get your company's logo digitized** in a format that can be inserted readily into Microsoft Word documents and templates. If it's not already in an accessible electronic format such as .TIF or .BMP, get your logo scanned in and touched up for clarity.

2) Pull out your offset printing bills for the past year or so and see where you're spending the most. This will help you prioritize your cost-saving potential. Then determine whether some of these outside printing jobs could be handled internally if your company, for example, purchased a special grade of paper for your laser printer or invested in a high-speed color laser printer. As a fellow small business owner, I know I'm constantly evaluating these cost-saving possibilities.

3) Assemble a team of Microsoft Word savvy staff members to begin drafting some templates. For the sake of consistency and branding, your staff should agree on a common set of formatting styles (fonts, sizes and so forth). If your documents look bland, vaguely resembling as much flair and pizzazz as something coming off an electric typewriter, get familiar with some of the included Microsoft Word templates and styles. Using these pre-fabricated design elements is not difficult, but is often the key difference between an amateurish and professional document appearance.

4) Don't format text by hand in Microsoft Word. Templates always include a set of preformatted styles, which you can easily modify or add to. As seen in Figure 3-4, you can find the Style drop-down list on the left side of the Formatting toolbar. Be sure to use styles in your Microsoft Word documents to ease your initial formatting and document maintenance.

Figure 3-4

Professionally designed styles give your documents a sense of flair and consistency, while easing maintenance burdens.

Keeping Employees on the Same Page

To ensure consistency within your company, place newly customized and created Microsoft Word templates (.dot files) in a folder on your file server that all employees have access to.

Then, under the Tools menu, Options command, File Locations tab, select Workgroup Templates. Then Modify and select the shared template folder location (Figure 3-5).

Tip:
To maintain greater centralized control, you may want to give read-write permissions to these files only to designated managers. Everyone else could get read-only permissions.

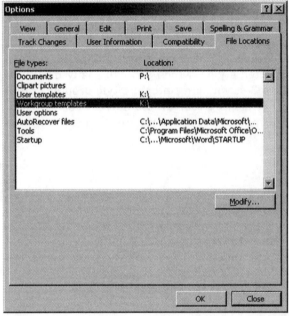

Figure 3-5

By pointing all employees' Microsoft Word configurations to the same Workgroup Templates folder on your server, you can ensure that everyone has the same version of Microsoft Word templates available when choosing the File, New command.

Tip #48

Standardize your file formats to ensure companywide compatibility.

✓ **Save on Soft Costs**

✓ **Save on Out-of-Pocket Expenses**

Standard File Formats Bridge the Gap

By standardizing on a common set of applications and file formats companywide, you easily can drive down your computer support costs. In large companies, this very subject can stir up hours of heated internal debate. However, don't overlook a *huge* benefit of being small: It's a *lot* easier and quicker to make across-the-board changes, and *much* easier to keep everyone on the same page, figuratively and literally.

In many companies, it's fairly common to find several different word processing and spreadsheet programs. It's also *highly* likely your firm is running at least two, possibly three or more, versions of Microsoft Office programs. Unlike Microsoft's upgrade from Microsoft Office 95 to Microsoft Office 97, which introduced major changes to the underlying document file formats, the upgrades to Microsoft Office 2000 and Microsoft Office XP bring *much* more subtle, conservative changes.

Avoiding the Purchase of Unnecessary Version Upgrades

As a result, you do not need to upgrade all of your PCs to the same version of Microsoft Office applications to standardize on a single set of file formats. An across-the-board upgrade would be an expensive proposition. Usually, version upgrades can be phased in gradually as new PCs that include bundled versions of Microsoft Office are purchased.

To get the compatibility benefits, you merely need to standardize the file format selections in use. This becomes a cinch as Microsoft Office 2000 and Microsoft Office XP offer integrated support for Microsoft Office 97 file formats. For all applications except Microsoft Access, there is basically full backward compatibility with Microsoft Office 97.

Before making any changes to the underlying file formats you use, or upgrade your Microsoft Office applications, you always should make sure you have at least one verified and tested full system backup. For more cost-saving tips on data backup, see Chapter 6.

Microsoft Word .doc Files

For example, if you have four PCs with Microsoft Word 2000 and eight PCs running Microsoft Word 97, you can make the documents compatible with one another by toggling a simple dialog box choice.

To do so, in Microsoft Word 2000 go to Tools, choose the Options command, then click on the Save tab (Figure 3-6).

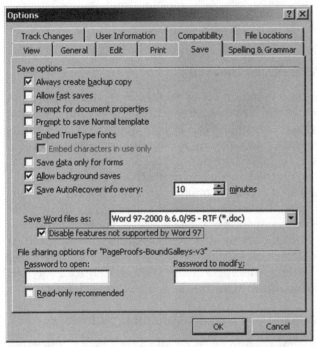

Figure 3-6

Don't run up big support bills because of incompatible file formats across different versions of Microsoft Word. Make the configurations compatible by changing two simple settings in the Microsoft Word 2000 Tools, Options, Save dialog box.

In the middle of that dialog box, you'll see a drop-down list called "Save Word files as:"

From there, change the default selection of Word Document (*.doc) to Word 97-2000 & 6.0/95 – RTF (*.doc).

Finally, enable the check box immediately below to "Disable features not supported by Word 97."

When you're finished, simply click OK.

If you want employees to be able to create documents compatible with earlier versions of Microsoft Word, set this configuration choice on *each* PC.

Microsoft Excel .xls Files

Microsoft Excel 2000 and Microsoft Excel 2002 have similar features that make workbooks backward-compatible with earlier versions of Microsoft Excel.

Just as with Microsoft Word, start at the Tools menu and choose the Options command.

Click on the Transition tab as seen in Figure 3-7. Toward the top of that dialog box, you'll see a drop-down list labeled "Save Excel files as:"

Now change the default Microsoft Excel Workbook selection to Microsoft Excel 97-2000 & 5.0/95 Workbook. Then click OK.

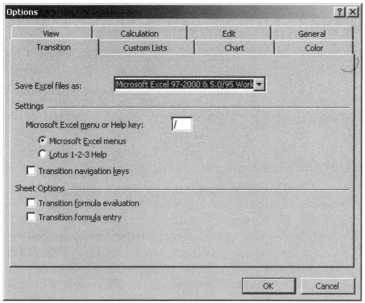

Figure 3-7

Prevent expensive Microsoft Excel workbook compatibility problems by configuring backward file format compatibility on each PC running Microsoft Excel 2000 or Microsoft Excel 2002.

Just as with Microsoft Word 2000, this configuration choice can take your files all the way back to 16-bit versions of Microsoft Excel (circa 1994).

Learn once – apply many places

The more you use Microsoft Office applications, the more you'll realize the undeniable benefits of learn once, apply many places. Here we see huge similarities when changing default file format settings in both Microsoft Word and Microsoft Excel.

With *tremendous* consistencies across applications, you can learn one skill set and be able to apply that skill set to many other applications. Ultimately, once you've developed proficiency in one Microsoft Office application, you'll be able to learn the next program *much* more quickly.

Your trip up the learning curve is dramatically accelerated, courtesy of several important and universal features, such as common Toolbar buttons, pull-down menus and dialog boxes.

Microsoft Publisher .pub and Microsoft PowerPoint .ppt Files

Microsoft Publisher 2000 can back save to Microsoft Publisher 98 files directly from the Save As dialogue box, "Save as Type" drop-down list.

Microsoft PowerPoint 2000 provides similar backward file format compatibility options under its Tools menu, Options command, Save tab.

Microsoft Access .mdb Files

Microsoft Access 2000 and Microsoft Access 2002 are bigger challenges. When Microsoft Corporation upgraded Microsoft Access 97 to Microsoft Access 2000, it changed the underlying database engine. If you have several employees who use an important Microsoft Access database, you'll likely need to standardize on one version of Microsoft Access, as opposed to relying on file format configuration settings.

Microsoft Access 2000 cannot share a common file format with Microsoft Access 97, but Microsoft Access 2000 *can* save a database in Microsoft Access 97 format.

Glossary:
Have you visited this book's Glossary yet? Get a quick refresher on over 160 terms used throughout this book -- all those buzzwords and acronyms frequently thrown around by computer consultants and other techies. The Glossary, with extensive cross-references and chapter references, begins on page 231.

Sharing files when Microsoft Office isn't available

Sharing Microsoft Office files with Apple Mac OS users once was difficult. However, recent versions of Microsoft Office for Macintosh and transferring files easily through e-mailed file attachments have made this a distant memory.

However, there still may be times when end users you support need to exchange files regularly with vendors or clients who don't have Microsoft Office. Fortunately, Microsoft Office offers one more built-in option: HTML.

The language of Web pages, HTML (hypertext markup language) is fully supported in Microsoft Office applications and is a *powerful* and flexible addition.

For starters, if your employees are creating Microsoft Office 2000 or Microsoft Office XP documents destined for internal or external Web servers, there's no need to spend time converting documents back and forth between native Microsoft Office file formats and HTML.

Second, once a document is saved in HTML format, anyone with a modern Web browser or HTML-enabled e-mail program can view the document, just as if that person had Microsoft Word or Microsoft Excel installed on his or her PC. This basically has made the concept of free Microsoft Office viewers obsolete.

Tip #49

Appoint one person in charge of server folder structure and file-naming conventions.

✓ **Save on Soft Costs**

Save on Out-of-Pocket Expenses

Avoid Productivity-Sapping Chaos

Implementing a local area network (LAN) is one of the easiest ways to scale up from personal productivity to workgroup or companywide productivity.

However, once employees begin sharing file folders on a centralized file server, chaos can follow *rapidly*.

If you're looking for an analogy in the offline world, consider what would happen if you bought a new lateral file cabinet and told *everyone* they could put whatever they wanted in it, without any underlying structure (no drawer labels, no hanging folders, no nothing).

Four Steps to Organizational Success

As a result, it's very important to appoint an owner of each shared-file folder. This person gets four key responsibilities.

1) **Design and maintain** an orderly set of folders and subfolders
2) **Monitor** storage space use (checking the MBs and GBs)
3) **Purge and archive** obsolete folders and files
4) **Set up and enforce** file-naming conventions everyone can follow easily

This job is usually a good fit for a department manager, supervisor or team leader. The folder captain doesn't necessarily need to be *that* computer-literate, but does need to be very well-organized and detail-oriented.

Many small businesses assume that the internal guru or computer consultant can handle these tasks. However, by the time storage space is running low or folders have become an out-of-control mess, it's usually an unwelcome emergency task that easily can be avoided by taking the above proactive steps.

Tip #50

Treat all unexpected Microsoft Office files e-mailed to you as virus suspects.

✓ **Save on Soft Costs**

Save on Out-of-Pocket Expenses

Microsoft Office viruses, mainly those that attack Microsoft Outlook (and to a lesser extent Microsoft Word and Microsoft Excel) are *prolifically* prevalent and destructive. Worse yet, a virus will strike when you least expect it to.

Innocent until proven guilty?

This is *not* a good approach to dealing with Microsoft Office documents that appear in your e-mail Inbox.

Instead, unless you *specifically* know that the file is coming, you should handle *every* unsolicited Microsoft Word and Microsoft Excel file you receive in your e-mail Inbox as suspicious, even if the file comes from someone you know.

Computer viruses can be *very* expensive to clean up once they've infiltrated your company. We'll look at antivirus software and best practices in more detail in Chapter 8. But for now you should at least know that any Microsoft Word or Microsoft Excel file that's e-mailed to you that you weren't expecting, no matter who it's from (even from a boss, spouse or computer consultant), should be looked at with a *strong* degree of virus containment skepticism.

Third-Party Assistance

In addition to keeping your third-party antivirus software up to date daily or weekly, Microsoft provides many Microsoft Office-specific security patches that, among other things, help to protect you from viruses.

Microsoft Assistance

The Microsoft Office Product Updates Web page offers an easy way to keep up with the latest Microsoft Office patches, enhancements and service releases. Visit office.microsoft.com/ProductUpdates/

Tip #51

Use the Detect and Repair feature to prevent expensive technical support and computer consultant service calls.

✓ **Save on Soft Costs**

Save on Out-of-Pocket Expenses

First introduced in Microsoft Office 2000, the Detect and Repair command on the Help pull-down menu (Figure 3-8) automatically fixes both file and Registry-level problems with Microsoft Office applications.

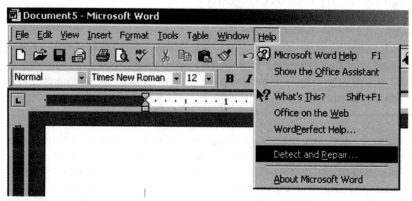

Figure 3-8

Use the Microsoft Office Detect and Repair feature to attempt to correct technical glitches on your own, before spending money to call for technical support or your local computer consultant.

Note:
The Registry is a hierarchical database used to store configuration information for user preferences, installed hardware, operating system configuration choices and software application settings. Every version of Microsoft Windows since Microsoft Windows 95 relies on a Registry. Because the Registry is like the central nervous system of software, you must make sure it is backed up regularly. For more money-saving data backup tips, see Chapter 6.

A cornerstone of Microsoft's self-repairing, self-healing benefits powered by the Windows Installer Service, Detect and Repair automatically searches for missing or corrupted files and then automatically repairs them.

Resource Directory:
Want an easy way to recall the over 60 Web site references discussed in this book? Check out the Resource Directory, starting on page 261, for suggested Web sites that deal with PC hardware and peripherals, software applications and operating systems, data protection and other general small business technology information.

When you run Detect and Repair, you'll usually be asked to insert the appropriate Microsoft Office CD-ROM. Even so, the *huge* leap forward here is that there's *almost* no need for complex, manual troubleshooting.

Note:
Keep track of which Microsoft Office CD-ROM you used for each installation. Aside from needing to manage this in excruciating detail for software licensing purposes, any Detect and Repair operations or patches you apply to Microsoft Office may fail, if you don't have the original CD-ROM available.

Tip #52

Get familiar with the built-in maintenance and repair tool for Microsoft Access.

✓ **Save on Soft Costs**

Save on Out-of-Pocket Expenses

Mention the buzzwords, "relational database," and many small business managers' eyes glaze over at the prospect of maintaining and repairing their Microsoft Access database. Don't let the thought of these tasks intimidate you. Maintaining and repairing a Microsoft Access database isn't much more difficult than those things you already know about other Microsoft Office applications.

Crucial Backups

Before I introduce you to this key utility that can prevent an emergency technical support or computer consultant call, you need to do a nightly verified and regularly tested backup of *any* Microsoft Access databases at your company. If you have a *very* low tolerance for data loss, you even may want to back up more than once a day.

In Part III, we'll look at all kinds of data protection measures you can take to prevent expensive, devastating database corruption. But, for the time being, backing up a Microsoft Access database regularly should be a top priority.

Maintenance 101: Compacting and Repairing a Database

Relational databases run best when all the tables are indexed properly, the way you can look up information in a book quickly by referring to a properly designed index in the back.

Microsoft Access does a decent job of keeping these indexes up to date on its own. This alone is a huge improvement over previous generations of relational database programs. However, as various items in a database (tables, queries, reports, forms, fields and records) are added and removed, space builds up between data that makes using the database less efficient.

This dilemma is very similar in concept to the way a hard drive becomes fragmented. To eliminate disk fragmentation, you'd run a defragmentation utility. In Microsoft Access, the process is called compacting.

Note:
Before running this utility program on a Microsoft Access database, make sure all users are out of the database, *and* that you have a current verified and tested backup copy.

To run the Compact and Repair operation on a Microsoft Access 2000 database, go to the Tools menu, choose the Database Utilities command, followed by the Compact and Repair Database command on the submenu (Figure 3-9). In most cases, Microsoft Access takes care of the rest, without complications.

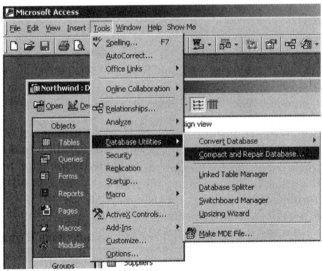

Figure 3-9

The Compact and Repair Database command in Microsoft Access can be used to optimize and repair a database.

Tip:
If you want to see what kind of impact compacting has on the size of your Microsoft Access database, open Windows Explorer and look at the size of the .mdb file before and after you run the utility program.

If your Microsoft Access database application is split between two .mdb files, where one contains the data tables and the other contains the front-end, you'll need to run the Compact and Repair process on each .mdb file separately.

Tip #53

Learn to use two simple maintenance and repair tools for Microsoft Outlook.

✓ **Save on Soft Costs**

Save on Out-of-Pocket Expenses

Just as with Microsoft Access databases, Microsoft Outlook Personal Folders (.pst files) can become bloated and inefficient, as well as corrupted or damaged.

Crucial Backups

As with Microsoft Access, be sure your Personal Folders File is backed up and verified *every* night. Again, if you have a very low tolerance for data loss, consider backing up more often than once a day. (Chapter 6 offers more tips on implementing a cost-effective, easy-to-maintain, data backup regimen.)

The "Corporate or Workgroup" version of Microsoft Outlook 2000 has a very straightforward utility for compacting your Personal Folders File (.pst). And, just as when you compacted Microsoft Access .mdb files, you can get an idea of the impact of this operation by inspecting the .pst file size, both before and after compacting. Once again, you can find file size information through Windows Explorer.

Tip:
To learn whether you're running the "Corporate or Workgroup" version of Microsoft Outlook 2000, go to the Help menu and choose the About command.

Compacting a Personal Folders File

To compact your Personal Folders File, first exit out of Microsoft Outlook. Then, from your Start menu, go to Settings, and then Control Panel.

Within the Control Panel, open the Mail applet. Then, select the Personal Folders entry and click the Properties button, as you'll see in Figure 3-10. Finally, in the Properties dialog box, click the Compact Now button. Microsoft Outlook will take over from there. Do *not* interrupt this operation while the file is being compacted.

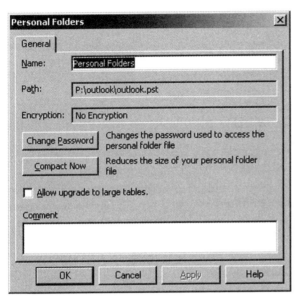

Figure 3-10

Although a Microsoft Outlook Personal Folders File (.pst) can become bloated, the Compact Now button allows you to remedy this problem easily.

While you're in this dialog box, for future reference record the file name and path of the Personal Folders File in Table 3-5.

Microsoft Outlook Maintenance Planner

	Inbox Repair Tool (Scanpst.exe)	Personal Folders (*.pst)
Location on My Computer (drive letter: \folder\filename)		

Table 3-5

To run the Inbox Repair Tool, you'll need to know the file path location of both the Inbox Repair Tool and the Personal Folders File. Use Table 3-5 to record these file path locations.

When compacting is complete, click OK and then another OK to close the Mail applet. Then close the Control Panel.

Inbox Repair Tool

Sometimes, instead of just compacting for the sake of proactive maintenance, you may get an error message that prevents you from opening your Personal Folders when you launch Microsoft Outlook. If you've already tried obvious troubleshooting steps (rebooting your PC and making sure you're logged on properly), try the Inbox Repair Tool.

Because the Inbox Repair Tool utility program and Personal Folders File often end up in various locations on different PCs, the first step is to find the Inbox Repair Tool. So let's first open Windows Explorer, also known as Exploring Windows or Windows NT Explorer.

Right click on My Computer and choose the Search or Find File command. To find the Inbox Repair Tool, we'll search for the file named scanpst.exe, as you'll see in Figure 3-11. Then record the folder path of scanpst.exe in Table 3-5 earlier in this section. The full path and file name of your Personal Folders File (.pst) already was recorded in Table 3-5 when you compacted the Personal Folders File earlier in this section.

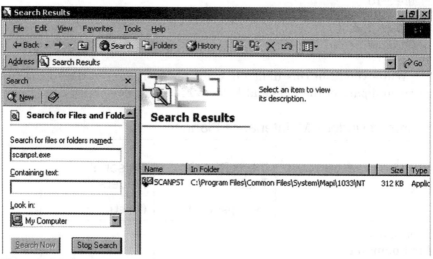

Figure 3-11

Before you can run the Inbox Repair Tool for Microsoft Outlook, first determine where its scanpst.exe file is on your hard drive.

To launch the Inbox Repair Tool, double click on the scanpst.exe file that you found a few moments ago. Then, as you see in Figure 3-12, click the Browse button to select the location of your Personal Folders File (.pst) we identified earlier.

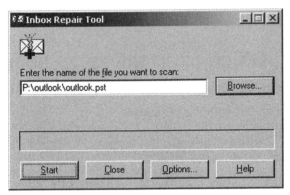

Figure 3-12

Before you can click Start, first enter the name and path of the Personal Folders File you want to scan.

Next, click the Start button and allow the Inbox Repair Tool to do its magic. Take great pains to make sure this process doesn't get interrupted midstream, as this may result in *severe* data corruption. After the Inbox Repair Tool scans through your Personal Folders File (eight steps), you'll get a progress report (Figure 3-13) and an opportunity to back up your Personal Folders File before proceeding.

When you're ready to continue, click the Repair button to complete the process. Once finished, you will be asked to click OK to acknowledge that the repair process is complete.

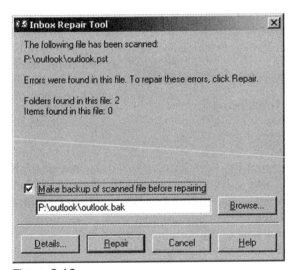

Figure 3-13

Before the Inbox Repair Tool goes into Repair mode, you'll get a brief summary of results and the opportunity to view Details of findings.

Tip #54

Survey Microsoft Office alternatives.

✓ **Save on Soft Costs**

✓ **Save on Out-of-Pocket Expenses**

No look at cost-saving techniques for Microsoft Office could be complete without at least presenting some other options. Because Microsoft Office commands somewhere near 90 percent market share in many of the software categories it competes in, you cannot put much stock in any other products and companies as viable commercial possibilities. However, at least you'll be aware you have a choice.

- **Corel WordPerfect Office 2002** – includes Word-Perfect, Quattro Pro, Corel Presentations, CorelCENTRAL, Paradox and Dragon Naturally-Speaking -- www.corel.com
  Relative Cost Indicator: $$-$$$

- **Lotus SmartSuite Millenium Edition 9.6** – includes Lotus Word Pro, Lotus 1-2-3, Lotus Freelance Graphics, Lotus Approach, Lotus Smart-Center, Lotus Organizer and Lotus FastSite -- www.lotus.com
  Relative Cost Indicator: $$-$$$

- **Sun StarOffice 5.2** – includes word processing, spreadsheet and presentation applications -- www.sun.com
  Relative Cost Indicator: $

Know What You're Up Against

If you are considering switching to one of these suites, you need to factor in all the less obvious soft costs, way beyond the purchase price.

First, you will have *tremendous* migration costs with testing and piloting, file conversion and training of administrators and end users.

Also, you will find nowhere near the number of third-party applications and add-ins written for these alternative products.

Finally, because most of your customers, suppliers and business partners have likely standardized on Microsoft Office, switching to another suite might make sharing files going forward much more difficult.

The Bottom Line

You can leverage Microsoft Office to lower your out-of-pocket expenses and more indirect computer support costs in many ways. In this chapter, we looked at some Microsoft Office-specific cost-saving tips you can put to work right away in your small business.

We saw how to streamline personal productivity and your company's workflow, eliminate redundancy and drive down outside printing costs.

Then we looked at ways to standardize file formats without big upgrade expenses and how to eliminate many technical support and computer consultant expenses for common problems such as file corruption, viruses, database and e-mail damage.

Resource Box

- **Corel** -- www.corel.com

- **Joshua Feinberg's Small Biz Tech Talk** -- www.smallbiztechtalk.com

- **Lotus** -- www.lotus.com

- **Microsoft Office** -- www.microsoft.com/office/

- **Microsoft Office Product Updates** -- office.microsoft.com/ProductUpdates/

- **Sun Microsystems** -- www.sun.com

Table of Tips:
Need a quick refresher on the 101 money-saving tips discussed in this book? Check out the Table of Tips, beginning on page 267, for a chapter-by-chapter recap and quick reference.

Companion CD-ROM

Are you ready to take your cost-savings to the next level, but you're at a loss for the *right* questions to ask? Check out the Companion CD-ROM for *What Your Computer Consultant Doesn't Want You to Know* -- with over 550 Action Items to get you started saving money right now.

The Action Items are presented in a variety of convenient file formats including Adobe Acrobat .pdf, HTML, Microsoft Word .doc and Microsoft Excel .xls. In addition, the Action Items are loaded up in a Microsoft Outlook Personal Folders File (.pst) -- ready for you to import into your Microsoft Outlook Tasks. The Companion CD-ROM also includes an electronic Resource Directory, recapping the book's suggested Web sites, that's all set for you to import into your Microsoft Internet Explorer Favorites list. Use the handy Action Item format to copy, paste and delegate -- while you tailor the money-saving program to your company's unique needs.

For more information on the Companion CD-ROM, see page 285.

Or visit www.smallbiztechtalk.com/tools/ to download sample Action Items or order the Companion CD-ROM.

Chapter 4
Microsoft Windows
on the Desktop

Consumer vs. Business Versions, Navigation,
Preventing System Crashes and Lost-File Panic,
Offline Files, Recovery, Obsolete Software,
Standardization, Testing and Documentation

In Chapters 1 and 2, we emphasized how to lower your small business computer expenses with PC hardware and peripheral devices. Then, in Chapter 3 we shifted gears to software and concentrated on cost-reduction opportunities with Microsoft Office.

Now, we'll spotlight some simple money-saving techniques you can use with the Microsoft Windows family of operating systems. With more than six versions of Microsoft Windows in use among small businesses, you have *plenty* of opportunities to save (and waste) money.

Let the games begin!

Tip #55

Evaluate whether you need features in business versions of Microsoft Windows.

✓ **Save on Soft Costs**

Save on Out-of-Pocket Expenses

Because everyone claims to know *something* about PCs today, you need to understand whether *and* why you *need* a business version of Microsoft Windows.

Avoiding System Crashes

Until Microsoft Windows XP Home arrived, previous versions of Microsoft's consumer operating systems still were based on *very* antiquated, 16-bit underpinnings. Microsoft Windows XP Home was the first consumer version of Microsoft Windows built on the enhanced Microsoft Windows 2000 kernel, which evolved from the Microsoft Windows NT kernel. The new kernel alone, the same one in Microsoft Windows XP Professional, is a quantum leap forward in reliability.

Tip:
The term kernel is used to describe the core internal services that power an operating system.

The consumer-oriented Microsoft Windows 9x product line *had* to be hybrid operating systems, combining both old and new operating system technologies, so Microsoft could guarantee backward compatibility with a full range of MS-DOS-based legacy software applications and hardware devices.

Note:
I use the phrase "Microsoft Windows 9x product line," to abbreviate and encompass three consumer-oriented operating systems: Microsoft Windows 95, Microsoft Windows 98, and Microsoft Windows Me, which share a common MS-DOS heritage.

Although the Microsoft Windows 9x consumer product line runs 32-bit software, these consumer versions of Microsoft Windows still retain many of the vestiges of their 16-bit DOS history.

Because Microsoft Windows 9x-based operating systems can run real mode device drivers very similar to those used under MS-DOS 6.x, the home user versions of Microsoft Windows are inherently *much* less reliable. The business versions of Microsoft Windows always have *required* native, 32-bit device drivers and, as a result, have been more crash-proof.

Tamper-Proofing the Security

Although the consumer-oriented Microsoft Windows 9x product line always provided the *illusion* of some local security, in reality it offered no protection. Worse yet, Microsoft Windows 9x products gave people a false sense of security. Even a beginner could compromise the Microsoft Windows logon.

Also, the business versions of Microsoft Windows allow you *easily* to set up controls to prevent curious users from tinkering with their software configuration. Anything like this you can do to prevent tampering will do wonders to lower your computer support costs.

Superior Underpinnings and Performance

Because of the underlying architecture of the Microsoft Windows 9x product line, a single buggy software application can crash your entire PC. With business versions of Microsoft Windows, most substandard software applications will *not* interfere with other software programs.

The business versions of Microsoft Windows also are more scalable. As you add more RAM, faster processors, and even a second processor, performance continues to increase.

Comparing Microsoft Windows 2000 Professional to Microsoft Windows NT Workstation 4 and Microsoft Windows 98

Independent studies have shown that Microsoft Windows 2000 Professional is faster *and* more reliable than Microsoft Windows NT Workstation 4 and Microsoft Windows 98. For example, ZD Labs found that:

Microsoft Windows 2000 Professional was 17 times more reliable than Microsoft Windows NT Workstation 4, and 50 times more reliable than Microsoft Windows 98.

Microsoft Windows 2000 Professional was 27 percent faster than Microsoft Windows 98, both with 64MB and 128MB of RAM.

Tip #56

Make sure your Microsoft Windows version was designed for the rigors of business use.

✓ **Save on Soft Costs**

Save on Out-of-Pocket Expenses

Don't get seduced by the low price of consumer versions of Microsoft Windows. Since 1995, Microsoft has had a two-tier product line. The lower-end, entry-level products tend to be *much* less reliable and are designed for consumers, while the premium operating systems are optimized for the demands of businesses.

Note:
Microsoft Windows XP Home was the first consumer operating system designed to put stability ahead of backward compatibility.

Not All Windows Are Created Equal

Although each new version added more bells and whistles, the stripped-down, low-budget version of Microsoft Windows always was intended for the casual home PC user.

However, even before the release of Microsoft Windows 95, Microsoft had a more dependable, secure and efficient operating system, Microsoft Windows NT, built for the more discriminating business user. Table 4-1 shows consumer and business operating systems used by most small businesses today.

Roll back your calendar to August 1995, when Microsoft Windows 95 shipped amid huge promotional fanfare. At the time, the PC hardware required to run the business version of the Microsoft Windows operating system, Microsoft Windows NT Workstation 3.51, just wasn't affordable for most small businesses.

However, in 1997, PC hardware prices began to plummet. This meant faster processors, larger hard drives, more RAM and speedy video graphics accelerators.

Even entry-level PCs became powerful enough to run Microsoft's flagship business operating system. Almost overnight, small businesses could afford to enjoy the *enormous* security, performance and reliability of the premium versions of Microsoft Windows.

So, when Microsoft Windows 98 came out, Microsoft started promoting Microsoft Windows NT Workstation 4 as the desktop PC operating system of choice for small businesses.

Are you using the right version of Microsoft Windows?

Consumer products (home user)	Business products	
	Desktop	Server
Microsoft Windows 95 Microsoft Windows 98 Microsoft Windows 98, Second Edition Microsoft Windows Millennium Edition (Me) Microsoft Windows XP Home	Microsoft Windows NT Workstation 4 Microsoft Windows 2000 Professional Microsoft Windows XP Professional	Microsoft Windows NT Server 4 Microsoft Windows 2000 Server Microsoft Windows .NET Server
Relative Cost Indicator: $	*Relative Cost Indicator:* $-$$	*Relative Cost Indicator:* $$$

Table 4-1

Eight 32-bit Microsoft Windows products have been used by small businesses since the mid-'90s -- and that's just on the desktop side of the typical office network.

Glossary:
Have you visited this book's Glossary yet? Get a quick refresher on over 160 terms used throughout this book – all those buzzwords and acronyms frequently thrown around by computer consultants and other techies. The Glossary, with extensive cross-references and chapter references, begins on page 231.

Tip #57

Get a business version of Microsoft Windows bundled with your new PC purchase.

✓ **Save on Soft Costs**

✓ **Save on Out-of-Pocket Expenses**

Today's entry-level PCs, even those in the $599 to $799 range, are *extremely* capable of running the business versions of Microsoft Windows with blazing-fast performance.

Best Bona Fide Deal in Town

Most PC manufacturers include the current consumer version of Microsoft Windows in their base offerings. However, you usually can upgrade when purchasing from a home user version of Microsoft Windows to a business version for around $100.

Compared to purchasing the upgrade at a later date, this is a *great* value.

Note:
In Chapter 5, we'll look at software licensing.

We already have seen how to save money on computer support costs by getting components, such as CD-RW drives and Ethernet adapters, bundled with the purchase of a new PC.

It's basically the same idea with bundled operating systems.

Besides the product purchase cost savings, you'll find *numerous* computer support-related reasons to get a business version of Microsoft Windows bundled with the purchase of a new PC.

Many times the deal is *so* sweet it pays to replace the entire PC just to get the bundled discount on the business version of Microsoft Windows, rather than purchase the full-packaged, shrink-wrapped product at a retail store.

Guaranteed Compatibility

By getting an operating system such as Microsoft Windows 2000 Professional bundled with your new PC purchase, you won't worry about whether the hardware works with the operating system, applications and utility software.

There's also no need to wonder whether the PC hardware components have stable device drivers written for your desired operating system.

The flip side: imagine upgrading to Microsoft Windows XP Professional a year after your PC purchase and discovering that you need to first buy new components – such as a new video card, sound card or tape backup drive.

Supported Configuration

When the operating system is preinstalled by the PC manufacturer, more than likely the company's technical support department will assist you in your time of need – such as when your PC crashes two hours before a key proposal is due!

The converse: Tackle the upgrade on your own later and you may endure the telephone equivalent of rolled-eyeballs and shrugged-shoulders indifference.

Time and Cost Savings

In case you've never had the experience of doing an operating system upgrade, this sort of project *easily* can take a half-day or more. And that's if everything goes reasonably smoothly.

So if you upgrade to a business version of Microsoft Windows later, instead of getting it bundled with your PC purchase, you may be courting trouble.

Either your internal guru will be stuck on this frustrating task for several hours, or your computer consultant will rack up several billable hours.

Or perhaps the worst of both worlds -- your internal guru gets stumped on the upgrade for several days. Then you *finally* call in the expensive computer consultant to bail out the internal guru.

Avoid these headaches from the start by having the business version of Microsoft Windows factory installed.

Table of Tips:
Need a quick refresher on the 101 money-saving tips discussed in this book? Check out the Table of Tips, beginning on page 267, for a chapter-by-chapter recap and quick reference.

Why operating system upgrades often take several hours

Are you still feeling brave enough to handle an operating system upgrade on your own, instead of getting the operating system factory installed on a new PC?

Every once in a while, you may get lucky and be able to complete a Microsoft Windows version upgrade in an hour or two. But don't count on it.

Consider *some* of the more common tasks that go into this kind of project.

- **Backing up** *all* data and making sure the backup is verified and tested.
- **Inventorying** *all* key software applications and hardware devices, then researching whether they're *supposed* to work under the new desired operating system.
- **Tracking down and purchasing or downloading** any required software applications, device drivers and firmware upgrades.
- **Deciding whether to perform a clean installation**, where you reformat the hard drive and start from scratch, or an in-place installation where you install the new version of Microsoft Windows on top of the old one. (A clean installation is generally preferable but typically more time-consuming than an in-place installation.)
- **Installing the operating system**.
- **Reinstalling or reconfiguring** software applications and hardware components.
- **Migrating user data** and preferences.

These are just *some* of the reasons you should have your PC manufacturer worry about many of these headaches *before* your PC leaves the factory.

Tip #58

Place your users' most important tools conspicuously on the Microsoft Windows Desktop.

✓ **Save on Soft Costs**

Save on Out-of-Pocket Expenses

In Chapter 3, we saw how Microsoft Office Toolbars, which are remarkably consistent across the entire suite of software applications, position your most commonly used commands in easy view.

Less Clutter = Fewer How-To Questions = Lower Support Costs

Although the power user still may need to venture occasionally into the pull-down menus to get to less commonly used commands, your core end users can be *much* more productive by primarily using Toolbars.

Because there is much less clutter and potential for confusion with Microsoft Office Toolbars, you'll end up with fewer "how-to" questions for your internal guru and virtually no need to contact an external technical support hotline or expensive computer consultant.

The Value of Desktop Shortcuts

The Microsoft Windows Desktop, across *all* modern versions of the operating system, provides a similar facility. Although some of your advanced users may savor the flexibility of navigating around the Start Menu to launch their applications, most of your end users are *much* better off having their handful of commonly used software applications appear as Shortcuts on the Microsoft Windows Desktop.

Again, just as with Microsoft Office Toolbars, this simplicity will go a long way toward reducing computer support costs. In Figure 4-1, you'll see a typical Microsoft Windows Desktop, with a handful of commonly used program Shortcuts.

Quick Launch Toolbar: One More Opportunity for Simplicity

In addition, Figure 4-1 contains four Taskbar Shortcuts in the bottom left of the screen, just to the right of the Start Menu button. This is called a Quick Launch Toolbar.

Tip:
The Taskbar is the area on the bottom of your screen between the Start Menu and Clock. Although the Taskbar can be moved to the top, left or right side of the screen, I don't recommend changing the default bottom of the screen position for PC beginners.

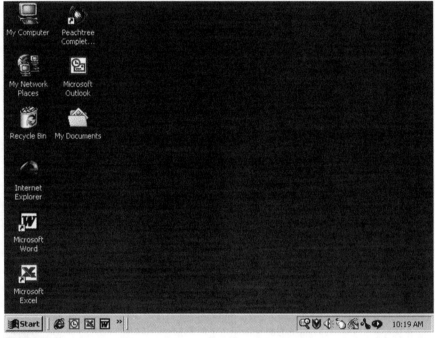

Figure 4-1

A typical Microsoft Windows 2000 Professional Desktop, with added Shortcuts for Microsoft Word, Microsoft Excel and Peachtree Complete Accounting.

If it isn't already on, you can enable the Quick Launch Toolbar by right clicking on the Taskbar. From there, select Toolbars from the context sensitive pop-up menu and make sure Quick Launch has a check mark next to it (Figure 4-2).

On the Quick Launch Toolbar, you'll notice single clickable Shortcuts for some popular programs, such as Microsoft Internet Explorer, Microsoft Outlook, Microsoft Excel and Microsoft Word, providing one more opportunity to put a few *very* commonly used software application Shortcuts directly in front of users. This once again can reduce dra-

matically the need to hunt around a crowded Start Menu – and ultimately eliminate many costly user requests for assistance.

Figure 4-2

By enabling the Quick Launch Toolbar on the Taskbar, you can place a few more commonly used program Shortcuts within easy striking distance of novice users.

Removing Unneeded Bundled Software Desktop Shortcuts

Major PC manufacturers often have the clout to cultivate lots of software bundling deals -- ultimately providing a *lot* of preinstalled software for the customer. But on brand-name PCs with bundled software, you'll often find Desktop Shortcuts for programs that either won't be used by your users, might confuse your users or require a high degree of technical expertise. If this is the case, remove the extraneous Shortcuts.

When desktop PCs and notebooks come bundled with lots of third-party utility software, it's *extremely* common to have four or five Shortcuts on a Microsoft Windows Desktop that are completely inappropriate for most users in your company. Customize end users' Desktops for individual needs. Don't tempt your average users with Shortcuts leading to programs that might cause inadvertent PC configuration damage.

Finally, if your users' Start Menus begin to get absurdly large and unwieldy, consider visiting the Add/Remove Programs applet in the Control Panel. There, you can remove any unneeded software applications that may be doing nothing other than creating confusion and potential costly support headaches.

Tip #59

Never turn off a Microsoft Windows PC until you're told it's safe to do so.

✓ **Save on Soft Costs**

Save on Out-of-Pocket Expenses

If you've been using Microsoft Windows operating systems for a while, this next best practice is probably *so* ingrained into your daily work habits you hardly give it a second thought.

Must Hear Training Topic for Your Supported PC Users

But users new to Microsoft Windows need to be trained, both during their initial computer orientation and reminded at regular intervals, *not* to turn off the power button on their PCs *until* Microsoft Windows tells them it's safe to do so.

Tip:
Some companies attempt to solve this problem by placing stickers near PC power buttons reminding users not to turn off their PCs until Microsoft Windows tells them to do so.

This may sound *really* basic, but for years I've seen small businesses incur truly substantial downtime and emergency computer consulting expenses because users either never were warned or forgot. However, here are two exceptions to this golden rule.

Automatic Power Off

First, many PCs and Microsoft Windows versions support power management standards that allow the operating system actually to turn off the PC automatically when you choose the Shut Down command from the Start Menu.

This convenience was initially a nice enhancement on notebook computers, but it now has filtered its way down to most new desktop PCs as well.

Problematic System Hang-ups on Shutdown

Second, many times a PC, particularly if running an operating system from the Microsoft Windows 9x consumer product line, *refuses* to gracefully shut down.

Rather, the PC stalls out on the "Please wait while shutting down" message. Instead of simply ignoring this condition and powering the PC off before they're told it's safe, your users should be trained to alert the internal guru or computer consultant to this problem so the real difficulty can be determined and fixed.

Not following these procedures can lead to a loss of unsaved data, operating system damage or complete PC boot-up failure.

Obviously, ignoring these best practices can be detrimental to your company's productivity and *extremely* harmful to your small business computer support costs.

Automated power off capabilities on PC hardware

For the automated power-off capability to work properly, both the operating system and PC hardware must support the Advanced Configuration and Power Interface (ACPI).

Microsoft's operating systems started widely supporting this standard around the time Microsoft Windows 98 was released.

ACPI support for PC hardware usually is built into the BIOS, a chip on your computer's main system board that acts as one of the main translators between the hardware and software worlds. You usually can find out whether a particular PC supports a certain level of ACPI-compliance by reading through the technical specs on the PC vendor's Web site.

For more background on ACPI, visit www.acpi.info and www.microsoft.com/hwdev/onnow/.

Tip #60

Let Microsoft Windows 2000 Professional and Microsoft Windows XP protect you from flaky software.

✓ **Save on Soft Costs**

Save on Out-of-Pocket Expenses

If you've ever endured the nail-biting, teeth-clenching experience of hoping that a third-party software application or hardware device didn't break a stable PC configuration, you'll love these reliability-enhancing improvements in Microsoft Windows 2000 Professional, Microsoft Windows XP Home and Microsoft Windows XP Professional.

Not a Perfect World

In a perfect world, every software and hardware vendor would rigorously test *all* of their products on *all* operating systems and service packs.

But, with more than a half-dozen current versions of Microsoft Windows on small business PCs, and the many service releases and service packs required to keep operating systems functioning reliably, there are lots of opportunities for vendors to drop the ball. Unfortunately, this carelessness in software integration, testing and quality assurance can cause *serious*, expensive computer support migraines.

The Value of Testing as Part of Your Due Diligence

Technology professionals routinely test *any* unknown piece of software and hardware in a controlled, simulated lab environment, *before* deploying it on mission-critical user systems. In larger companies with big Information Technology (IT) departments, these kinds of best practices are commonplace.

Note:
Before installing new software or hardware on a server, it is even *more* crucial to perform this kind of testing. Unlike a desktop PC, a crashed server easily could cripple your entire company.

In small businesses, where the only formal IT support is often from an internal guru or outsourced computer consultant, many times the due diligence is glossed over.

However, because installing a flaky piece of software or hardware can crash a PC, ignoring the need for testing can be a *huge* mistake. Until now, you could do little besides doing your homework, to protect yourself from this risk. Fortunately, Microsoft Windows 2000 Professional introduced a feature to protect the innocent.

Tools to Protect the Innocent

Windows File Protection can prevent one software vendor's files from overwriting another software vendor's key system files. Unguarded, this file egotism, especially when affecting a key operating system file in the crucial `..\system32` folder, can trash your PC configuration.

Making for a *much* more reliable PC configuration, Windows File Protection *automatically* prevents these critical files from being inadvertently replaced.

Device Driver Signing, also introduced with Microsoft Windows 2000 Professional, ensures that the hardware device drivers you are *about* to install have passed the Microsoft Windows Hardware Quality Labs testing. Or, alternatively, if the device drivers are not signed, you are warned.

Just as important, the Windows File Protection and Device Driver Signing can help save your small business from the *huge* expense of an emergency service call from your local computer consultant.

Resource Directory:
Want an easy way to recall the over 60 Web site references discussed in this book? Check out the Resource Directory, starting on page 261, for suggested Web sites that deal with PC hardware and peripherals, software applications and operating systems, data protection and other general small business technology information.

Tip #61

Help your road warriors save on long-distance telephone charges and frustration.

✓ **Save on Soft Costs**

✓ **Save on Out-of-Pocket Expenses**

How often does one of your mobile employees, equipped with a notebook computer and modem, have to dial into your office server to transfer files back and forth?

A Workaround for Slow, Unreliable, Exorbitant Hotel Dial-In

Usually these long-distance telephone calls show up on an expense report at hotel room telephone rates, which are generally very steep!

So, it's in your best interest to do *everything* you can to make sure your road warriors have *all* the files they need *before* they hit the road. But, how do you tackle the challenge of keeping files in sync with any changes made while traveling?

Synchronizing Your Files

Fortunately, Microsoft Windows 2000 Professional and Microsoft Windows XP Professional have a built-in feature to manage all this for you. The Offline Files feature, running in conjunction with Synchronization Manager, allows you to keep working with files and folders on a server, *even* when you have no physical connection to the server.

Note:
Only the business versions of Microsoft Windows support Offline Files.

So you don't need to establish a dial-up, LAN or virtual private network (VPN) connection. It's as if you've taken a network-mapped drive on the road with you.

Upon reconnecting to the server, Synchronization Manager synchronizes any file updates you have made while traveling with the appropriate server-shared folder.

The Offline Files Wizard

Setting up Offline Files is *very* straightforward.

In Windows Explorer, select the desired files and folders, right click and select Make Available Offline, then run through the Offline Files Wizard (Figure 4-3).

Just select the files you want to have available offline while you're still connected to the LAN. When you log off the LAN, Synchronization Manager transfers the files to your notebook. While traveling, you can work on the Offline Files as if you were connected to the LAN, even with the same mapped drive letters and folder paths.

Figure 4-3

The Offline Files Wizard is a great tool for road warriors who need to synchronize files on their notebook with files on server-shared folders. This often can eliminate the need to dial into the server over slow, hotel-grade telephone lines while traveling.

Returning to the Office

Then, when you return to the office and plug back into the LAN, Synchronization Manager synchronizes any changes you made while on the road with the appropriate files on the server-shared folder. No need to dial-in remotely.

With the Offline Files Wizard, there's no need to be subjected to unreliable, slow hotel telephone lines. And there's no need to rack up obscenely expensive long-distance charges.

Tip #62

Recover damaged configurations easier and faster with Microsoft Windows 2000 Professional and Microsoft Windows XP.

✓ **Save on Soft Costs**

Save on Out-of-Pocket Expenses

Anyone who ever has had to rebuild a PC configuration, wiping the drive clean by repartitioning and reformatting, can relate to the significant amount of time involved. You need to reload the operating system, redo the network configuration, reinstall the required device drivers and software applications, and apply any custom settings.

Avoiding the Agony of a Full System Rebuild

Before you start over, Microsoft Windows 2000 Professional and Microsoft Windows XP include some tools worth investigating. In Microsoft Windows 2000 Professional, the Recovery Console and Safe Boot Mode can save several hours of agony. In Microsoft Windows XP, the Automated System Recovery (ASR) Wizard and Safe Boot Mode can achieve approximately the same results.

Time-Saving Recovery Tools in Microsoft Windows 2000 and Microsoft Windows XP

By dramatically reducing the time required to fix many operating system problems, the Recovery Console allows you to check and repair your hard drive's boot sector and master boot record. The Recovery Console also helps you repair problems related to operating system services and devices. The Safe Boot Mode is very similar to the Safe Mode that's been around for years in the consumer Microsoft Windows 9x product line. With a Safe Boot Mode startup sequence, you can launch Microsoft Windows 2000 Professional with a minimal device driver and service configuration.

Both the Recovery Console and the Safe Boot Mode give you a *much* better chance of fixing a damaged configuration, *without* having to resort to a productivity hampering and expensive operating system rebuild. The Automated System Recovery Wizard, new to Microsoft Windows XP, goes a step further and actually monitors and logs system changes, to allow for automated rollback.

Tip #63

Prevent lost-file panic by training users on find-file searches.

✓ **Save on Soft Costs**

Save on Out-of-Pocket Expenses

As Microsoft Windows has become a more mature platform, PC users don't tend to get much operating system training anymore. Your users don't need to be experts on Microsoft Windows, but they *do* need to know some basics -- such as how to find a missing file.

More Must Hear End User Training

Just as *every* small business PC user should know how to recover a wayward Microsoft Office Toolbar, as we saw in Chapter 3, don't forget to train users on how to search for missing files. Because a lost document can cause panic that sets off a chain of events, often including an expensive emergency call to your computer consultant, you'll want to prevent these crises before they start by providing some targeted training.

Regardless of which versions of Microsoft Windows are in use at your company, Windows Explorer (also known as Exploring Windows or Windows NT Explorer) has remained relatively similar for many years. Here are some Windows Explorer basics to incorporate into your end user training.

Seven Steps to Fewer Panic Calls to the Consultant

1) **Show how to launch Windows Explorer**, through either the Start Menu or through a Desktop Shortcut, if you've created one for this purpose.

2) **Discuss how Windows Explorer allows you to view**, create, delete, manage, move and copy folders and subfolders.

3) **Demonstrate how the left panel shows drives, folders and subfolders**, and the right panel displays *individual* files within various drives, folders and subfolders.

4) **Explain the different drive letter conventions** in use at your company, encompassing both local and network drive mappings.

5) Show users how to reveal All File Details, so they can see not only the file name but also the file type, size and last modified date and time stamp.

6) Demonstrate how to sort on a file property by clicking once or twice at the top of the column in Windows Explorer. Let's say you've misplaced a Microsoft Excel file, but you have a pretty good hunch it's in a certain directory. However, with more than 400 other files there, you're having a hard time finding it. By choosing View, All File Details and clicking once or twice at the top of the Type column, you'll group all the Microsoft Excel Workbook files (.xls) together, making for easier visual inspection. If all 400 files in the folder are Microsoft Excel files, you could sort on the file size or date and time stamp to help find the lost workbook.

7) Demonstrate how to use the Find File or Search command to search on a file name, file type, file size, or file date and time stamp. For example, last summer you created a Microsoft Word file *somewhere* on your X drive. Now the file is missing. You can search on *.do?, encompassing Microsoft Word documents (.doc) and templates (.dot). Then add in a date range of perhaps May 1 to Oct. 1 of the relevant year.

You cannot possibly plan for every lost-file contingency, but your PC users should be armed with basic knowledge on how to hunt down any files they suspect have disappeared. This sense of empowerment will do *wonders* to reduce user anxiety *and* your computer support costs.

Free E-mail Newsletter:
Would you like a convenient way to keep up with new tips and techniques from Small Biz Tech Talk? Take control of your technology now! Subscribe to the free bi-weekly Tips newsletter at www.smallbiztechtalk.com

---

Tip #64

Retire your outdated software.

✓ **Save on Soft Costs**

✓ **Save on Out-of-Pocket Expenses**

Does your PC hardware, software and operating system inventory look like an exhibit from a computer museum?

Are you still running outdated software applications that were developed to be compatible with MS-DOS or 16-bit Microsoft Windows 3.1 technology?

Upgrading obsolete industry-specific software may seem like an incredibly expensive, time-consuming proposition, but staying with the status quo can be even more damaging to your small business computer support costs.

To make a more informed decision about these obsolete software programs, consider various support issues and expenses that are directly attributable to the aging software.

Then, when you're ready to scout for replacements, you'll have a few basic choices.

Option A:
Look to others in your industry for recommendations.

Relative Cost Indicator: $

Attend industry trade shows, talk to others in your industry and look in trade publications for leads on available software solutions.

Investigate online resources that may discuss industry-specific software, such as Internet search engines and directories, industry-specific Web sites and portals, and industry-specific message boards or newsgroups.

Option B:
Contract with a computer consultant to custom design a replacement from scratch.

Relative Cost Indicator: $$-$$$-$$$$

Consider hiring a local small business computer consultant to develop a custom database application, using an off-the-shelf program such as Microsoft Access.

Make sure any custom application approximates and improves on the functionality of your outdated software program.

Option C:
Contract with a computer consultant to help you evaluate various options.

Relative Cost Indicator: $$-$$$-$$$$

Retain the services of a computer consultant to evaluate your narrowed-down list of industry-specific solutions, from Option A, *before* you make the purchase decision.

Incorporate this independent, technical tire kicking as a key part of your overall due diligence.

For many small businesses, adopting a diverse research approach, borrowing ideas from Options A, B and C will work best.

Companion CD-ROM

Are you ready to take your cost-savings to the next level, but you're at a loss for the *right* questions to ask? Check out the Companion CD-ROM for *What Your Computer Consultant Doesn't Want You to Know* -- with over 550 Action Items to get you started saving money right now.

The Action Items are presented in a variety of convenient file formats including Adobe Acrobat .pdf, HTML, Microsoft Word .doc and Microsoft Excel .xls. In addition, the Action Items are loaded up in a Microsoft Outlook Personal Folders File (.pst) -- ready for you to import into your Microsoft Outlook Tasks. The Companion CD-ROM also includes an electronic Resource Directory, recapping the book's suggested Web sites, that's all set for you to import into your Microsoft Internet Explorer Favorites list. Use the handy Action Item format to copy, paste and delegate -- while you tailor the money-saving program to your company's unique needs.

For more information on the Companion CD-ROM, see page 285.

Or visit www.smallbiztechtalk.com/tools/ to download sample Action Items or order the Companion CD-ROM.

Tip #65

Use a clean installation to get a more stable, predictable PC configuration.

✓ **Save on Soft Costs**

✓ **Save on Out-of-Pocket Expenses**

Software Removal Routines Often Don't Succeed

Problems can be created and compounded by years of installing and uninstalling software.

Although these issues tend to be especially prevalent with older MS-DOS-based and 16-bit software programs, even some 32-bit applications have nonfunctional, nonexistent or ineffective uninstall routines.

How PC Performance and Reliability Deteriorates

By removing these layers of upgrade baggage, you can restore your system configuration to a clean state that approximates the condition, performance and reliability of the PC when it was manufactured.

Carefully Planned System Rebuilds Rejuvenate PCs

A clean installation or rebuild can bring a PC back to the pristine condition that approximates a new system, but it should *not* be done without careful planning and research.

Any operating system upgrade such as this easily can take a half-day or more to complete.

However, when the value of the hardware is still substantial, or if the PC is relatively new, in many cases this computer support expense is clearly justified.

Note:
For details on the steps involved in this kind of project, see the side-bar on "Why operating system upgrades often take several hours" earlier in this chapter (Tip #57).

141

Why hand-me-downs *need* to be handled as clean installs

The clean install approach to PC configurations can be a real lifesaver in managing PCs that move from person to person in your company as hand-me-downs.

In as much as this is a very common way to extend the asset life of PCs, you need to know how to do it right.

Let's say your CEO has a relatively high-end desktop PC that's about a year old. The CEO decides to go completely mobile and gets a notebook and docking station. The CEO's desktop PC gets passed down to an executive assistant.

Then, a year later, this executive assistant needs a PC with a 40GB hard drive for a streaming video application. So, you take the CEO's former PC off the assistant's desk and redeploy that PC to someone in the sales department, who has relatively simple software requirements.

A few months later, this salesperson goes on a brief maternity leave, after which she gets permission to telecommute full-time for another few months. The salesperson's PC now goes home with her. What's wrong with this picture?

The salesperson on maternity leave has a curious husband who one day stumbles upon a folder on the PC's hard drive with several Microsoft Excel workbook files. The workbooks are date and time stamped from about 18 months ago, around the time the CEO originally gave up the desktop PC. These Microsoft Excel workbook files contain a series of tables, listing year-end bonuses and salaries for everyone in the company for the past five years. Ouch!

Because you weren't yet a believer in clean installations, or perhaps didn't know how important they are, that fatal folder of sensitive workbooks *never* was cleaned out as the PC was moved from employee to employee.

Tip #66

Standardize your PC hardware purchases.

✓ **Save on Soft Costs**

Save on Out-of-Pocket Expenses

Small businesses often have a *very* diverse fleet of custom-assembled PCs, also known as clone or "white-box" systems. These PCs may have been assembled from components by an internal guru, purchased as complete systems from a local retail computer store or procured from mail order vendors.

Regardless, if you haven't been purchasing consistently through a top-tier, brand-name PC vendor, you've been making computer support *much* more difficult on yourself than it needs to be.

Free Online Resources That Save Time

Most major PC vendors have *excellent* self-service technical support Web sites, where you can enter a PC serial number or model number and get a complete list of all included hardware components, as well as updated documentation, firmware revisions and device drivers.

These online resources, generally available for desktop PCs, notebooks and servers, are *critical* time-saving tools when troubleshooting or upgrading a PC. *Without* these resources, or if the vendor has gone out of business, tracking down required device drivers and documentation can be anywhere from difficult to a *near impossible* scavenger hunt.

Avoiding Device Driver Scavenger Hunts

For various computer support tasks, you often need to find hardware device drivers for video cards, network cards, modems, sound cards, host adapters, CD-RW drives and tape drives. The board-of-the-month club approach, epitomized by much of the "white-box" PC industry, is great for your local computer consultant's profit margin and job security, but it can be extremely detrimental to your computer support costs in the long run.

If you've never been intimately involved in this kind of frustrating PC hardware work, consider yourself fortunate. But also recognize that these tasks can be painfully time-consuming, if you don't have PC hardware consistency and appropriate vendor resources at your disposal.

Tip #67

Test anything new before assuming it works.

✓ **Save on Soft Costs**

Save on Out-of-Pocket Expenses

If this is your first foray into computer support, you may wonder why any testing is necessary. After all, can't you just install a software program and hardware device and see whether it works?

In the old days, before 32-bit versions of Microsoft Windows, resolving troublesome software and hardware configurations was much, much easier.

Healthy Dose of Software/Hardware Paranoia

However, with newer versions of Microsoft Windows, all you need is one unstable software application, utility program or buggy piece of hardware to literally crash your Microsoft Windows PC configuration into oblivion. That's why the system protection and recovery enhancements in Microsoft Windows 2000 Professional and Microsoft Windows XP, which we discussed earlier in the chapter, are *so* crucial.

So, when dealing with hardware or software that is new to your company, you must rigorously test the product *before* installing it onto someone's PC.

The Hazards of Appeasing the Boss

For example, your CEO may be extremely eager for you to install a new contact management program that just came out.

But how would your CEO feel if, while you were installing the program, the notebook locked up, wouldn't reboot and took three days and a $500 computer consultant emergency service call to get the notebook back to its former working condition?

Note:
That scenario could be the same for any unknown peripheral device such as a handheld PC cradle, digital camera or scanner.

Cost-Effective Testing Options

One better option – you can run through the installation on a similarly equipped PC of someone who wouldn't mind if his or her PC got trashed. Perhaps that person is you, depending on the nature of your job. *Relative Cost Indicator*: $

The best choice is to maintain a spare or test system. This PC should be relatively similar, in terms of hardware, software and operating system configuration, to your standard PC. That way, if the new product breaks something, it's not disabling someone such as your CEO! *Relative Cost Indicator*: $$-$$$

If you're testing a network application, it's even better if you have a second test or spare system. This way one PC can simulate the workstation and the other can simulate the server. *Relative Cost Indicator*: $$$

If you don't have the resources for these spare or test systems in-house, a local computer consultant usually can provide testing services on an outsourced basis. *Relative Cost Indicator*: $$-$$$

At any rate, *always* assume that a program or device could be *big* trouble until you see it working properly on a similarly equipped system.

Tip:
Some internal gurus and IT professionals use their home PCs for testing new software and hardware. Just be sure the configuration is at least *relatively* similar to the standard configuration in your office. *Relative Cost Indicator*: $

Tip #68

Document your Microsoft Windows configurations.

✓ **Save on Soft Costs**

Save on Out-of-Pocket Expenses

If you seriously want to drive down your computer support costs, maintaining software configuration consistency is *just* as important as PC hardware standardization.

Consistency Breeds Predictability and Reliability

By applying the same desktop PC and notebook configuration settings across the board, you'll avoid reinventing the wheel *every* time you do a PC upgrade.

At the same time, your computer support predictability and reliability will improve dramatically.

A Valuable Troubleshooting Tool

By developing this configuration consistency into some kind of system documentation, you'll build up a checklist to use when troubleshooting problems. In addition, this checklist becomes invaluable when you're planning a major upgrade to the next version of Microsoft Windows. This documentation is also crucial for cross-training a second internal guru, or hiring a new computer consultant, if the need should arise.

Suggestions for Getting Started

This documentation does not even need to be a huge project.

You can start by consolidating and organizing all your notes on how you configure various PC hardware, software and networking products. Place these notes into a numbered, step-by-step Microsoft Word document or Microsoft Excel worksheet. Just as important, be sure to revise this living document periodically to reflect any changes to your company's PC standards.

For most small businesses, you'll likely have a slightly different set of configuration settings for each geographic location, such as your main office and any branch offices or field locations.

Tip #69

Investigate any viable desktop operating system alternatives to Microsoft Windows.

✓ **Save on Soft Costs**

✓ **Save on Out-of-Pocket Expenses**

The great majority of PCs worldwide run some 32-bit version of Microsoft Windows. However, there are two other well known desktop operating systems, with a small number of *extremely* loyal fans.

- **Apple Mac OS** -- www.apple.com/macosx/
  Relative Cost Indicator: $$-$$$

- **Linux** – A type of UNIX operating system called Open Source, Linux was developed and continues to be expanded by many individuals, companies and organizations worldwide. Although there are several distributors, I have no single Linux vendor of choice to recommend. To jump-start your search, Yahoo! has a very well-organized directory of hundreds of Linux-related Web sites at dir.yahoo.com/Computers_and_Internet/Software/Operating_Systems/UNIX/Linux/ .
  Relative Cost Indicator: $

Just as with substitutes for Microsoft Office we saw in Chapter 3, you need to be aware of the hidden soft costs of switching to one of these Microsoft Windows alternatives.

First, consider the tremendous time and resources your company would need to devote to training, testing and piloting a substitute for Microsoft Windows, if you gave serious thought to switching.

Then, think about all of the third-party hardware devices, software applications and utility programs your company relies on. How many of these vendors even have an equivalent product outside the realm of Microsoft Windows? And if there are options, what will these third-party products cost your company as you migrate everything over to another operating system?

The Bottom Line

With the many incarnations of Microsoft Windows, you can take plenty of steps to help reduce your overall support costs. Without applying some of these best practices, you can end up spending a small fortune on emergency operating system mishaps. Use the concepts discussed in this chapter to overhaul the ways your company deals with the many expenses related to Microsoft Windows.

Resource Box

- **Apple Mac OS X** -- www.apple.com/macosx/

- **ACPI Power Management** -- www.acpi.info

- **Joshua Feinberg's Small Biz Tech Talk** -- www.smallbiztechtalk.com

- **Linux related Web sites (Yahoo! directory)** -- dir.yahoo.com/Computers_and_Internet/Software/Operating_Systems/UNIX/Linux/

- **Microsoft OnNow and Power Management** -- www.microsoft.com/hwdev/onnow/

- **Microsoft Windows 95** -- www.microsoft.com/windows95/

- **Microsoft Windows 98** -- www.microsoft.com/windows98/

- **Microsoft Windows 2000** -- www.microsoft.com/windows2000/

- **Microsoft Windows Me** -- www.microsoft.com/windowsme/

- **Microsoft Windows NT Workstation 4.0** -- www.microsoft.com/ntworkstation/

- **Microsoft Windows XP** -- www.microsoft.com/windowsxp/

Chapter 5
Software Purchases and Maintenance

Application Service Providers, Bundled Software, Evaluating Planned Software Purchases, Site Licenses and Updating Software

In Chapter 3, we looked at ways to use Microsoft Office to drive down your computer support costs and related out-of-pocket expenses. Then, in Chapter 4, we examined money-saving techniques you can use with the many incarnations of the Microsoft Windows operating system.

Now we'll round out our look at software support cost control by surveying how small businesses buy, customize and update Microsoft Office and Microsoft Windows.

Tip #70

You probably don't want to be an early adopter of ASP-based software applications.

✓ **Save on Soft Costs**

✓ **Save on Out-of-Pocket Expenses**

When Internet use started growing exponentially in the mid-'90s, software vendors, financial analysts and Internet Service Providers (ISPs) began hyping a new business model called the Application Service Provider (ASP).

Looking Beyond the Sales Pitch

By contracting with ASPs, small businesses no longer would need to purchase, install, customize, troubleshoot, maintain or upgrade complex software applications. Rather, small firms would pay a monthly fee, and possibly a setup or installation charge, to an ASP that would host the desired software application on an outsourced basis on the ASP's server.

All, or nearly all, computer support tasks would be taken care of by the ASP, with presumably a large, well-trained 7-by-24 IT department. Small businesses would need only to arrange for reliable, high-speed Internet access.

ASP Appeal to Software Vendors

Software vendors such as Microsoft also loved the idea. With such mature products as Microsoft Office and Microsoft Windows, Microsoft felt that software subscriptions would transform a one-time purchase into an annuity. And Microsoft was hardly alone. In the small business accounting software space, Intuit, Oracle and Peachtree all jumped in as early promoters of the ASP concept.

The sales pitch for rentable software as a service sounds great -- on the surface. After all, small businesses were comfortable outsourcing their Web site and e-mail hosting to ISPs. So wouldn't it be the next evolutionary step to outsource an accounting or contact management program? Not so fast!

Financial Realities

In early 2001, Gartner Dataquest (www.gartner.com) predicted that about 60 percent of ASPs would be out of business by early 2002. Thus far, Gartner Dataquest's forecasts have appeared dead-on. What brought this about?

And why wouldn't small businesses be more enthusiastic about the prospect of turning their software headaches over to someone else?

Security Concerns and Lack of Affordable Broadband Internet Access

For starters, small businesses were rather leery of handing over confidential data to another firm. And what could be more highly prized than customer or financial records?

High-profile hacker attacks, although rarely made on ASPs, also have shaken confidence in storing sensitive information on someone else's servers.

Second, even the most efficiently tuned ASP-based, or hosted applications, assume that businesses have reliable, high-speed Internet access. For a while, DSL-based Internet access seemed to be the crucial catalyst for small businesses to warm up to the ASP way of doing things. DSL was *supposed* to provide reliable, broadband Internet access, at small business-friendly prices.

Tip:
DSL is short for digital subscriber line, an economical way of running high-speed telecommunications services over standard copper telephone wiring.

Importance of DSL to the ASP Industry

However, even those who qualified for DSL, based on geographical location, grappled with tremendous frustration and delays while waiting for DSL service to be activated.

In early 2001, as major independent DSL providers stumbled on extreme financial difficulties and suddenly shut down, small businesses were left stranded without Internet access.

As with ASPs, DSL providers' *tremendous* startup costs spiraled out of control faster than revenue growth.

Many expect that the major U.S. telephone companies will eventually become the dominant players in affordable, widespread, DSL Internet access.

However, for now, small businesses are forced either to go back to the Stone Age of dial-up Internet access or plunk down $500 a month or more for a traditional fractional T1 or Frame Relay based Internet access account.

Either way, the lack of widespread, affordable, high-speed Internet access *and* concerns about data security on external servers have hampered and will continue to prevent more extensive adoption of software as a service.

Unless you have some rather exceptional circumstances, steer clear of rentable software, at least for now.

Companion CD-ROM

Are you ready to take your cost-savings to the next level, but you're at a loss for the *right* questions to ask? Check out the Companion CD-ROM for *What Your Computer Consultant Doesn't Want You to Know* -- with over 550 Action Items to get you started saving money right now.

The Action Items are presented in a variety of convenient file formats including Adobe Acrobat .pdf, HTML, Microsoft Word .doc and Microsoft Excel .xls. In addition, the Action Items are loaded up in a Microsoft Outlook Personal Folders File (.pst) -- ready for you to import into your Microsoft Outlook Tasks. The Companion CD-ROM also includes an electronic Resource Directory, recapping the book's suggested Web sites, that's all set for you to import into your Microsoft Internet Explorer Favorites list. Use the handy Action Item format to copy, paste and delegate -- while you tailor the money-saving program to your company's unique needs.

For more information on the Companion CD-ROM, see page 285.

Or visit www.smallbiztechtalk.com/tools/ to download sample Action Items or order the Companion CD-ROM.

Tip #71

If you do lease software as a service, take precautions.

✓ **Save on Soft Costs**

Save on Out-of-Pocket Expenses

Given that more than half of the once high-flying ASPs are expected to go out of business shortly, if they haven't already, what can you do to protect your small business if you're already under contract with an ASP, or just have to try out software as a service?

The Hazards of Fly-by-Night ASPs

As with any major purchase of technology products or services, you need to do your homework. And if the contract value you're considering is substantial enough, or significant enough to your business, get your attorney and a qualified computer consultant involved in reviewing the ASP's contract and proposal.

Because of the high risk of financial distress, plan from the outset that your ASP will go out of business someday.

Entrusting Your Data to the Financially Troubled

Then decide what sorts of daily controls and procedures you'll put into place to protect your company's data and minimize downtime when your hosted application no longer is available.

Also, it's not enough just to check customer references. Don't forget to ask how daily maintenance and support tasks are handled. Inquire about basic data backup and restoration procedures, power protection, security and firewalls, virus protection and Internet backbone redundancy.

Tip #72

Get Microsoft Office and business-class Microsoft Windows bundled with a new desktop PC or notebook.

✓ **Save on Soft Costs**

✓ **Save on Out-of-Pocket Expenses**

So, if leasing software as a service from an ASP still is not ready for prime time, what *can* you do in the meantime to get the best value on your software purchases and minimize associated computer support costs?

Three Ways to Buy Microsoft Office or Microsoft Windows

Here are three prevalent ways small businesses acquire Microsoft Office and business-class versions of Microsoft Windows desktop software.

- Retail purchase

- Bundling with a new PC purchase

- Site license

Given Microsoft's clout in the software industry, consider its three basic offerings as a proxy for how most competing independent software vendors (ISVs) now distribute their software programs.

Note:

For an overview of the differences between consumer and business versions of Microsoft Windows, see Chapter 4. The current shipping business-class versions of Microsoft Windows are Microsoft Windows 2000 Professional and Microsoft Windows XP Professional.

Software Bundled with Desktop PCs and Notebooks: For Many Small Businesses, the Best Deal in Town

Major PC vendors -- such as Compaq, Dell, Gateway, Hewlett Packard and IBM -- routinely offer Microsoft Office and Microsoft Windows as bundled options.

Just as we saw in Chapter 1 the *huge* and compelling advantages of getting various peripheral devices bundled with the PC purchase, PC software bundling is an *extremely* cost-effective way to obtain the latest versions of Microsoft Office and business-class versions of Microsoft Windows.

Bundled Software as a Key Driver of PC Hardware Selection

In addition to bundled costs substantially lower than retail purchase prices, there are some *extremely* compelling reasons to get your desired software included with the purchase of a new PC. In fact, even if the implied bundled costs were relatively close to retail prices, the savings in soft costs should still sway your decision *strongly* in favor of bundled software.

Because this soft cost savings is *so* significant, it should dictate where you ultimately purchase your PC. For example, if you're buying your PCs from a local retail store or obscure mail order vendor that cannot match the value of software bundling provided by the major PC vendors, you're probably paying too much for computer support. Even if the initial PC purchase price differential *was* significant, say $100 or more, you'd still lose out on the *much* greater soft cost considerations if you don't leverage bundled software.

Lots of Soft Cost Savings Too

So what *are* the advantages of getting Microsoft Office and business-class Microsoft Windows bundled with a new PC purchase, as opposed to buying the software a la carte and doing your own upgrades?

Because of the potential technical support frustration, and costs of expensive computer consultants, any one of these benefits should make the decision a no-brainer. Many times these four benefits can very persuasively tip the scales in favor of replacing an aging desktop PC or notebook with a new system.

No Compatibility Risk

The PC vendor already has tested all the pieces, so you know the combination of PC hardware, peripherals, application software and operating system software all will work together correctly right out of the box.

You won't need to consult compatibility charts or surf all over the Web to find, download and install device drivers and update patches.

Newer Hardware with a Product Warranty

Rather than upgrading a component or two piecemeal, such as adding more RAM or replacing your hard drive, a new PC purchase brings *all* critical hardware components up to date *and* provides an accompanying new purchase warranty. If your computers are more than two or three years old, or out of warranty, replacing computers is generally a *much* more cost-effective solution.

Timesaving

By the time you get done upgrading hardware components and sitting through an operating system and software application upgrade, you *easily* will have spent a half-day or more on the project.

Regardless of whether you're factoring in your internal guru's workload or a computer consultant invoice, the major PC vendors can absorb this labor into their pricing structure *much* more efficiently. Major PC vendors have automated these processes so your potential half-day of work takes no more than a few minutes on their factory assembly line.

Recourse

If something goes wrong, actually more likely *when* something goes wrong, your PC vendor *shouldn't* have many outs for finger-pointing when *everything* in your PC came from them. You'll be able to contact your PC vendor's technical support department, either by phone or through online avenues, for assistance.

Tip:
Even when Microsoft Office and Microsoft Windows are preloaded on your desktop or notebook PC, be sure your PC vendor supplies installation media and unlocking keys. These two items can be crucial lifesavers if you need to troubleshoot or reinstall misbehaving software programs.

Tip #73

If you cannot justify the purchase of new PCs to get bundled software, consider Microsoft Open License.

✓ **Save on Soft Costs**

✓ **Save on Out-of-Pocket Expenses**

If your company doesn't want *or* cannot afford to buy newer PCs with bundled software, here is another cost-saving option to paying retail: Microsoft Open License (www.microsoft.com/licensing/).

With this program, the only caveat is that you need a minimum initial purchase of software licenses for five PCs. For small businesses with fewer than five PCs, stick with the bundled approach described in Tip #72, if possible.

Paying Retail: Worst of All Worlds

You may be accustomed to buying computer software and hardware products the same way you purchase other office equipment, such as desks, chairs, fax machines and paper shredders.

However, there is a *much* less expensive way to acquire Microsoft Office and Microsoft Windows software than purchasing shrink-wrapped software boxes at the local office supply superstore.

Tip:

For real world examples of the pricing advantages of Microsoft Open License, check out **Buying Microsoft Office XP via Open License Delivers Small Business Savings** at
www.smallbiztechtalk.com/news/archives/tips073001-ms1.htm
Outside of the USA, you can find details on Microsoft pricing and availability on the Microsoft Worldwide Web site at
www.microsoft.com/worldwide/

Besides a 10 to 20 percent initial out-of-pocket savings compared to retail purchases, Microsoft Open License also can help you save money on computer support costs.

Easier Control Over Media and License Agreements

Because you get a consolidated license agreement document and only purchase as much media as you need, it's a lot easier to keep your valuable software assets locked up.

This way, you don't have to worry about entrusting the software boxes to employees, or about expensive software assets walking off the premises.

Less User Tinkering and Tighter Anti-Piracy Control

With the license agreement and media under centralized control, presumably with your internal guru or another manager, users won't be able to pop in the installation CD and experiment.

Users also are prevented from sharing the software with others in the company who aren't authorized or licensed to run that program.

Easier Storage and End-of-Life Disposal

In areas where real estate is extraordinarily expensive and garbage disposal costs are high, consider the physical burdens of traditional software purchases.

With Microsoft Open License, it's a lot easier to manage and ultimately dispose of a few sets of media, than potentially dozens of boxes of shrink-wrapped software.

Table of Tips:
Need a quick refresher on the 101 money-saving tips discussed in this book? Check out the Table of Tips, beginning on page 267, for a chapter-by-chapter recap and quick reference.

Tip #74

Subject any proposed purchases of industry-specific software to a rigorous technical and business evaluation.

✓ **Save on Soft Costs**

✓ **Save on Out-of-Pocket Expenses**

For the past several years, I've seen countless small businesses waste *enormous* sums of money trying to find the perfect vertical software application for their particular industry. In Chapter 4, we looked at computer support considerations with outdated industry-specific software. Now let's look at some evaluation criteria for a *new* industry-specific software application your firm is considering purchasing.

Consider how the proposed software program fits in with your investments in Microsoft Office and Microsoft Windows.

In addition, find out how the software compares to what you've come to expect as standard amenities from software programs -- such as importing, exporting, context-sensitive help, pull-down menus and toolbars.

Have your internal guru or computer consultant perform a technical evaluation of the proposed software.

So, before you get all excited about some slick marketing presentation you saw at a trade show, a glossy direct-mail piece that landed on your desk, or a persuasive trade magazine ad that caught your eye, be sure to perform some due diligence on the software vendor and its product.

Assign a representative user or set of users to evaluate the proposed software purchase for business value.

Once you're satisfied that the proposed industry-specific software program is technically sound, consider the program's business value. Turn the program over to a few representative users in your company. Ask them to evaluate it from the standpoint of solving specific business problems.

In managing these pilot tests for small businesses, I've seen abysmal results when doing technical evaluations of proposed purchases of industry-specific software. So, rarely does software even get to the stage of end user business value testing. However, it's much better to find out if the program is a dog with fleas *before* you've written the nonrefundable check to the software vendor.

A few other words of caution to consider:

- **Avoid nontechnical salespeople.** For many years, I've seen dozens of industry-specific products verbally misrepresented by borderline computer-literate sales staff. If you have any doubts about the product's technical capabilities, *insist* on speaking to someone at the vendor who *is* technical.

- **Be watchful for obsolete technology.** If you're used to purchasing software from major software vendors, such as Adobe, Symantec and Microsoft, you may be shocked to find that small, industry-specific software vendors are years behind the curve.

- **Don't settle for a demo.** You need to kick the tires – ask for the real program.

- **Find out whether the software vendor is committed** to enhancements and upgrades. The program may be great today but seem really passé years later if no upgraded version becomes available.

- **Watch out for 32-bit Window-dressing covering up a 16-bit program.** Many times you'll find that a small industry-specific software vendor has tried to update an aging 16-bit software program by upgrading select parts of it to 32-bit code.

Tip:
Need help sniffing out the stench of a 16-bit impostor? In many versions of Microsoft Windows, the Processes tab of the Windows Task Manager yields big clues. To reach the Windows Task Manager, press Ctrl + Alt + Del and select Task Manager. On the Processes tab, red flag *any* occurrences of WOWEXEC or NTVDM. Also be wary if the Setup program won't install to a folder with a long file name, greater than eight characters – another telltale sign of 16-bit relics.

Tip #75

Prepare a safety net before installing software updates.

✓ **Save on Soft Costs**

Save on Out-of-Pocket Expenses

In a few moments, we'll look at software maintenance to keep your software running at peak performance, without having to rely exclusively on a computer consultant.

But, before we do that, here are a few things to be prepared for:

Half-Baked Software Revisions

First, the huge majority of software updates are useful and safe to install.

For the past few years though, Microsoft and other prominent software vendors have managed to let a few software updates out the door that weren't quite ready for daily use.

Such problematic updates taught most software vendors to more rigorously beta test *all* updates, but the rush to market nature of software development often hinders software quality.

Avoid the Bleeding Edge

You can avoid some of this risk by waiting a few weeks before installing any updates that have been *very* recently released.

Let the IT professionals in large companies endure the pain of bleeding-edge software updates, while you sit back and wait for the dust to settle.

Besides waiting a few weeks, what else can you do to minimize inherent risks with software updates?

Backups Rule

Always make sure you have *at least* one or two full, verified and tested system backups before installing updates.

Along the same lines, if you're running a PC with Microsoft Windows NT Workstation 4, be sure your Emergency Repair Disk (ERD) is also current.

Resource Directory:
Want an easy way to recall the over 60 Web site references discussed in this book? Check out the Resource Directory, starting on page 261, for suggested Web sites that deal with PC hardware and peripherals, software applications and operating systems, data protection and other general small business technology information.

Test and Start Slowly

If you have a similarly configured spare or test system, or even a PC at home, that's not considered mission-critical, start by installing the update on the less crucial PC.

And then proceed slowly, until you build more confidence, with a companywide deployment.

You're better off taking a little longer and having one angry user with a broken PC configuration, than the wrath of your entire company.

Don't assume that a software update is innocuous until you've proven it yourself.

That's why you first should install any planned software updates on a spare or non-essential system.

Glossary:
Have you visited this book's Glossary yet? Get a quick refresher on over 160 terms used throughout this book – all those buzzwords and acronyms frequently thrown around by computer consultants and other techies. The Glossary, with extensive cross-references and chapter references, begins on page 231.

Tip #76

Learn how to maintain your Microsoft Office software.

✓ **Save on Soft Costs**

Save on Out-of-Pocket Expenses

The days of being able to install a piece of software and let it sit unchanged for years are long gone.

Such software vendors as Microsoft continually release new software updates that warrant your attention.

Sometimes these interim updates fix documented bugs. Other times these updates improve performance, repair security vulnerabilities or add new features.

Free Updates – Really!

Many small businesses are not aware that Microsoft frequently issues free interim updates to its Microsoft Office family of products, in between major product version upgrades.

So if you have Microsoft Office 97 or Microsoft Office 2000 running on your PC and it was purchased from a retail store, or bundled with a new PC purchase, there's an excellent chance that your software is out of date.

Does this mean you need to spend money to upgrade to Microsoft Office XP to get current? Absolutely not!

Microsoft Office Product Updates Web Site

Microsoft issues free minor updates to its Microsoft Office products monthly, even sometimes weekly.

How can you find out about these updates and get them incorporated into your installation of Microsoft Office?

Point your Web browser to the Microsoft Office Product Updates at office.microsoft.com/ProductUpdates/ (Figure 5-1).

When you first reach the Microsoft Office Product Updates Web page, a detection engine wizard will scan your system for installed Microsoft Office products and recommend various critical updates, based on its findings.

Microsoft Office Download Center Web Site

Besides the Microsoft Office Product Updates, the Microsoft Office Download Center (Figure 5-2) at office.microsoft.com/Downloads/ also can be quite useful for maintaining Microsoft Office.

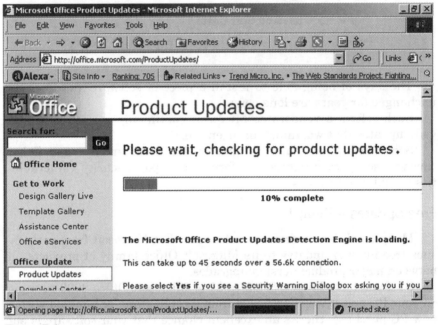

Figure 5-1

The Microsoft Office Product Updates Web site helps keep your Microsoft Office software current, without having to rely on a computer consultant.

To navigate through the Microsoft Office Download Center, first select whether you want updates to all the Microsoft Office suites, or updates for just a specific suite component, such as Microsoft Word.

On the Version drop-down list, you can choose either All Versions, 97/98, 2000 or 2002/XP.

In the example in Figure 5-2, I selected Updates, Add-ins and Extras, and Converters and Viewers for Microsoft Word 2000. When I click the Update List button, the Microsoft Office Download Center displays a list of available downloads for my indicated criteria. Note that the query results are displayed in descending date order, with the most current downloads listed first.

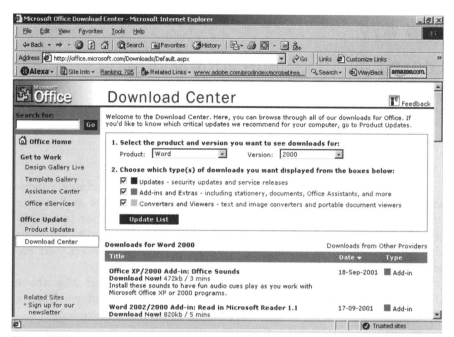

Figure 5-2

You can pick up additional software updates and add-ins for Microsoft Office at the Microsoft Office Download Center.

Tip:
You also can signup for a free e-mail subscription to the Microsoft Office Tools on the Web Update at www.microsoft.com/office/

Tip #77

Learn how to update your Microsoft Windows software.

✓ **Save on Soft Costs**

Save on Out-of-Pocket Expenses

Just as Microsoft Office gets a recurring stream of updates, Microsoft continually issues critical updates, hot fixes, patches and service packs for the Microsoft Windows operating systems. Similar to the Microsoft Office Product Updates Web page, the Microsoft Windows Update Web page (windowsupdate.microsoft.com) helps keep your operating system functioning securely, reliably and efficiently.

Besides reaching Microsoft Windows Update through the above URL, most versions of Microsoft Windows include a Windows Update Shortcut toward the top of the Start Menu, as seen in Figure 5-3.

Figure 5-3

Microsoft Windows 2000 Professional has a Shortcut toward the top of the Start Menu that allows you to launch Windows Update quickly.

System Scan and Recommendations

In much the same way the Microsoft Office Product Updates Web page inventories your PC so it can offer you the most relevant suggested downloads, Windows Update does a quick scan of your installed operating system, critical updates, hot fixes and service packs so it can recommend useful downloads.

Windows Update displays available product updates for the Microsoft Windows operating system and Microsoft Internet Explorer Web browser. While it is checking for available product updates, you'll get notification that your PC is being inventoried, as seen in Figure 5-4.

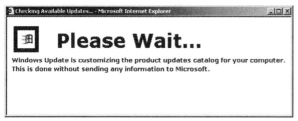

Figure 5-4

Windows Update does a quick scan of installed software on your PC so it can recommend relevant product updates.

Once Windows Update is done scanning your PC, you either can select new downloads, get a list of currently installed updates (Show Installed Updates), see a rundown of what's been installed and when (Installation History), or set personal preferences for using Windows Update (Personalize). These choices are shown in Figure 5-5.

Software Available on Windows Update

Recommended downloads are grouped into five categories.

- **Critical Updates** – You either can download and install Critical Updates conveniently as a consolidated, single installation package, or click on the + (plus sign) next to Show Individual Updates to obtain more flexibility.

- **Picks of the Month**

- **Recommended Updates** – As are Critical Updates, these are based on the software inventory Windows Update acquired during the scan a few moments ago.

- **Additional Windows Features**

- **Device Drivers**

Tip:
If you're looking for an easy way to be notified about new Windows Update downloads, subscribe to the free Microsoft TechNet Flash e-mail newsletter at www.microsoft.com/technet/

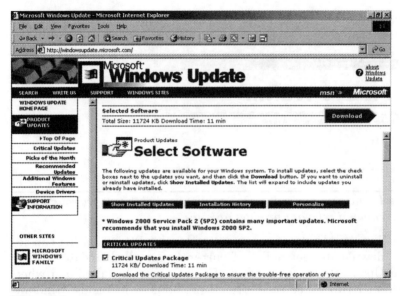

Figure 5-5

Windows Update effectively takes the place of a computer consultant by reviewing your installed update history and offering recommended options.

Critical Update Notification

Microsoft has a feature in Windows Update called Windows Critical Update Notification, which constantly monitors the Windows Update Web site for the availability of new crucial updates.

When one is available, you are notified and prompted to install the critical update.

However, this feature has a dark side.

By being among the first to install new critical updates, you're taking on *huge* early adopter risks that put your PC configuration out there on the bleeding edge.

I generally prefer to wait a minimum of three to five days for the dust to settle before installing any newly released software patch.

Tip #78

Know where to get other software updates.

✓ **Save on Soft Costs**

Save on Out-of-Pocket Expenses

Microsoft has such strong market share domestically and globally, so visiting the Microsoft Office Product Updates and Windows Update Web pages should satisfy *most* of your software maintenance needs.

With other software vendors, you generally can get to similar download centers through each vendor's Web site tech support area.

For example, if you need to keep Symantec software products up to date, you can find a button for Downloads right on its home page at www.symantec.com.

Once you're at the Symantec Downloads page, you might want to add this Web site address (www.symantec.com/downloads/) to your Bookmarks or Favorites list.

Similarly, Adobe has a Support link right on its home page at www.adobe.com, which takes you to the Adobe CustomerFirst Support Web site at www.adobe.com/support/.

From there, you'll see a hyperlink to File Downloads at www.adobe.com/support/downloads/, which you also may want to add to your Bookmarks or Favorites list.

For more software download listings that cover both commercial software updates and shareware from hundreds of smaller software vendors, consider visiting these two major software download portals.

- **CNET Downloads** -- download.cnet.com

- **ZDNet Downloads** -- www.zdnet.com/downloads/

The Bottom Line

Until a few years ago, you could purchase a software program, install it and assume that it would run fine as is for years. Just as the Internet has made it much easier for you to keep your software current, the dynamic nature of the Internet also *mandates* the need for perpetual software updates. But there's also no reason you can't save some money and handle most of this maintenance on your own, *without* the need to call a computer consultant.

We started this chapter by seeing how renting software as a service, from Application Service Providers (ASPs), has potential, but isn't yet recommended for most small businesses. Next, we discussed the pros and cons of two money-saving substitutes to buying Microsoft software at retail outlets: getting it bundled with the purchase of a new PC and entering into a license agreement.

In the second half of Chapter 5, we looked at ways to evaluate any planned purchase of industry-specific software, as well as measures to prepare your safety net *before* installing software updates. We closed out the chapter with an overview of ways to maintain Microsoft Office, Microsoft Windows and third-party software programs.

Resource Box

- **Adobe Downloads** --
  www.adobe.com/support/downloads/

- **CNET Downloads** -- download.cnet.com

- **Compaq Computer** -- www.compaq.com

- **Dell Computer** -- www.dell.com

- **Gartner Dataquest** -- www.gartner.com

- **Gateway** -- www.gateway.com

- **Hewlett Packard** -- www.hp.com

- **IBM** -- www.ibm.com

- **Joshua Feinberg's Small Biz Tech Talk** --
  www.smallbiztechtalk.com

- **Microsoft Licensing (Open License)** --
  www.microsoft.com/licensing/

- **Microsoft Office** -- www.microsoft.com/office/

- **Microsoft Office Download Center** --
  office.microsoft.com/Downloads/

- **Microsoft Office Product Updates** --
  office.microsoft.com/ProductUpdates/

- **Microsoft TechNet Flash** --
  www.microsoft.com/technet/

- **Microsoft Windows Update** --
  windowsupdate.microsoft.com

- **Microsoft Worldwide Sites** --
  www.microsoft.com/worldwide/

- **Symantec Downloads** --
  www.symantec.com/downloads/

- **ZDNet Downloads** -- www.zdnet.com/downloads/

Free E-mail Newsletter:
Would you like a convenient way to keep up with new tips and techniques from Small Biz Tech Talk? Take control of your technology now! Subscribe to the free bi-weekly Tips newsletter at www.smallbiztechtalk.com

Part III

Data Protection
Cost-Saving Tips

Chapter 6

Data Backup

Chapter 7

Power Protection

Chapter 8

Virus Protection

Chapter 6
Data Backup

Automation, Testing, Monitoring, Media Rotation,
Permanent Archives, Special Software Needs,
Physical Security, Purchase Options,
Online Backup and Scheduled Replication

According to IDC (www.idc.com), roughly 80 percent of small business and home office PC users have crucial data on desktop PCs and notebooks that are *not* backed up regularly.

When looking at data backup best practices, you'll find only two kinds of small businesses: those that have experienced a data disaster and those that will. Countless studies have shown that small businesses without a sound backup and disaster recovery procedure never fully recover. In addition, small businesses without a thorough, regularly tested recovery plan are likely to go out of business within a few months after a data disaster.

Ignoring basic disaster recovery planning can be very dangerous to your company's survival. Just because your company is a *small* business doesn't mean it's immune to *big* data disasters.

As do your Fortune 1000 counterparts, you probably have several mission-critical software applications running on your PCs and network. Without full-time IT staff however, your company may be considerably more vulnerable to a major IT disaster than you even realize.

As information becomes increasingly digitized and highly concentrated, planning for data disasters becomes more important than ever. Often the greatest threat isn't the potential for a data disaster to occur, *but* rather the *pervasive* denial that a disaster ever could happen to you.

In Part III, we'll round out our journey with money-saving techniques you can apply to data protection.

These will include simple precautions that must be taken to guard the enormous value of your company data against risks such as accidental and malicious file deletion, data corruption, unreliable utility power and viruses.

You'll learn the insider secrets of ways to plan your data protection *without* having to depend exclusively on an expensive computer consultant.

We'll begin Chapter 6 on data backup by surveying recommended technologies, planning, implementation and best practices.

In Chapter 7, we'll examine protecting your hardware and technology infrastructure from the dangers of unreliable utility power.

Then, in Chapter 8, we'll wrap up with an overview of virus prevention, in particular, how you can save money on *huge* soft costs by taking a more proactive role.

Tip #79

Know the pros and cons of various backup options.

✓ **Save on Soft Costs**

✓ **Save on Out-of-Pocket Expenses**

You can buy a wide range of backup system hardware and technologies for your small business. Choosing the right backup system can make an enormous difference in determining how bulletproof your company's technology backbone is. Select the wrong kind of backup system and you may end up with either a false sense of security, a system that relies heavily on manual steps or a computer support nightmare. Take your choice!

The Diskette Drive: Woefully Inadequate

***Relative Cost Indicator*: $**

At the absolute minimum, most PCs purchased by small businesses come with a built-in backup device, which uses *extremely* inexpensive media and is universally accepted.

So why don't more people use 3.5-inch diskette drives for backups? For starters, they're *very* slow, relatively unreliable and extremely limited in capacity (1.44MB).

Moreover, backing up a 20GB hard drive that's a mere 20 percent full would take about 2,800 diskettes -- making it *highly* unlikely that such a ridiculously cumbersome process would be repeated with enough regularity and consistency to be effective. Under the best-case scenario, diskettes can be used *occasionally* to back up a handful of individual data files, such as a few Microsoft Word documents (.doc) or Microsoft Excel (.xls) workbook files.

Note:
Many small business managers *think* the Iomega Zip Drive is a backup drive. However, the relatively high media costs, slow performance and limited 100MB to 250MB capacity make the Iomega Zip Drive a cumbersome tool with largely the same limitations as using a diskette drive for system backups.

The CD-RW Drive

Relative Cost Indicator: $-$$

The next option for small businesses, in terms of increasing price and fitness for the job, is the CD-RW drive. A very low-budget option, a CD-RW drive provides a relatively easy way for a small business to get up to 700MB of data onto a single media unit, which also is *very* inexpensive. In fact, CD-R and CD-RW media can hold roughly the equivalent of 450 diskettes. Even better, as are diskettes, CD-Rs are *very* universal and generally can be read on most standard CD-ROM drives.

So what's the downside? Even with up to 700MB of capacity, CD-RW backup systems are virtually inadequate for full system backup requirements of even today's entry-level PCs, which generally include 20GB or 40GB hard drives. So, at best, you could use CD-R or CD-RW media to backup data files but generally not programs.

However, most small businesses tend to have substantially more than 700MB of data files, even with just a handful of users. So even if you were to automate the backup of select data files to CD-R or CD-RW media, it's highly unlikely that 700MB of backup capacity would be adequate for the long term, even for a one- or two-person company.

And, if your backup system relies on switching out media during the backup process, it's unlikely the backup process will be carried out persistently as needed. All things considered, a CD-RW based backup system only can be used for *extremely* small microbusinesses, with unusually small data file storage requirements.

Travan Tape Drive

Relative Cost Indicator: $$-$$$

The next option for small business backup solutions is the first option discussed here that's actually feasible and recommended, albeit for a relatively small company. Entry-level tape backup drives, based on Travan technology, are generally a viable option for a stand-alone PC, small peer-to-peer network or home office.

Travan tape drives have many advantages. For one, the cost of the tape drive hardware is certainly within the affordable price range for a small business (typically $200 to $400). Travan-based tape drives, with 10GB to 20GB of storage space, also have ample capacity for most relatively small office storage requirements. This means you won't have to change the backup tape mid-job, dramatically increasing your chances of consistent success. Travan tape drives are also relatively reliable.

There are some critical downsides with Travan tape drives, though. For one, although the backup drives are relatively inexpensive, the backup media cost of about $30 to $40 is roughly 50 to 75 percent more expensive than comparable backup media for DAT tape drives, which we'll discuss in a moment.

So if you plan to implement my recommended 20-tape rotation, as well as permanent monthly archive tapes, you need to factor in the cost of buying 32 Travan tapes at once. If you're thinking this sounds a lot like the penny-wise, pound-foolish issue with inkjet printers we looked at in Chapter 2, you're quite right. A Travan tape drive is the relatively inexpensive part; the Travan media are where the costs start to soar.

Second, although Travan tape drives are *much* faster than backing up to diskette or CD-RW media, Travan tape drives still are substantially slower than DAT tape drives, which we'll look at momentarily. If you have a somewhat narrow window (say between midnight and 5 a.m.) when you can take a system offline for a full system backup, you need to consider the overall speed of the backup and verify jobs.

Consider **Seagate Technology** (www.seagate.com) as a starting point for researching the purchase of a Travan tape backup drive.

DAT Tape Drive: The Preferred Small Business Solution

Relative Cost Indicator: $$$

For small businesses with more than a few users and typical small business storage requirements, I always recommend the preferred server-grade solution, a DAT tape drive, which is based on digital audiotape media.

Although an internal DAT tape drive can run as much as $1,000 or more if purchased a la carte, the big PC vendors offer DAT-based tape drives as an option with server purchase for around $700 to $800. For most of the soft cost reasons we reviewed in Chapter 1, it *always* makes sense if possible to have the PC vendor factory install the tape drive into the server.

So although the DAT tape drive can cost two to four times as much as a Travan tape drive, the DAT-based tape drive is generally the best value for a small business with a dozen or more network users.

Note:
The value proposition of DAT tape drives is actually very similar to the lower cost-per-page idea of networked, workgroup laser printers that we explored in Chapter 2.

If you'll be purchasing 32 or more tape cartridges initially, you'll appreciate that DDS-4 (20/40GB) tape cartridges for DAT drives not only have a higher capacity and smaller form factor, but are actually *much* less expensive ($15 to $25). Compared to purchasing 32 Travan tapes at $30 to $40, the cost differential can be *tremendous*.

DAT tape drives are also *much* faster. Although performance varies by model and manufacturer, a DDS-4 based DAT tape drive can be as much as twice as fast on backup, verify and restore jobs as a Travan-based tape drive. Again, if you have only a four- to six-hour daily window for full system backups, speed becomes critical.

Finally, DAT tape drives are virtually silent, but Travan tape drives tend to make a whirring noise while operating. If the server is locked up and only running jobs overnight, this won't be an issue. But, it is worth pointing out, if the server happens to be on your desk and you're planning to run backup jobs during your business day.

To avoid configuration, device driver and compatibility headaches, while saving some money compared to retail, get the backup drive pre-installed with the purchase of a new PC or server.

Consider the following vendors as a starting point for researching the purchase of a DAT tape backup drive.

- **Hewlett Packard** -- www.hp.com

- **Seagate Technology** -- www.seagate.com

Note:

If you have an *unusually* large data storage requirement (well in excess of 20GB) or a bottomless budget, the next step up from DDS-3/DDS-4 DAT tape drives is DLT (digital linear tape). DLT-based tape backup drives are much faster and have more storage capacity, but these drives are generally too expensive for most small companies. *Relative Cost Indicator:* $$$$

Troubleshooting a DAT-based tape backup drive

If you have an internal DDS-3 or DDS-4 tape drive, you *occasionally* may have a tape that's stuck in the drive. The first sign of this: You press the eject button repeatedly and the tape still won't eject from the drive.

I've found that power cycling the drive almost always solves this problem. The trouble, however, is that for an internal drive, you'll actually need to shut down the server, power the server off briefly, then start it up again.

Everyone will need to be closed out of files on the network drives when you do this, so this is best accomplished at a relatively low-network utilization time, such as early morning, lunchtime or end of day.

Certainly, other backup options are on the market. However, most are based on proprietary backup media formats. I've installed, configured and supported dozens of implementations of all the backup system options discussed in this section. Each has its own unique advantages and disadvantages. For a comparison between Travan and DAT tape backup drives, see Table 6-1. Just be sure you're fully informed of the issues *before* you bet your business on one kind of solution.

Comparing Travan and DAT Tape Backup Drives

	Pros	Cons
Travan (TR-5) Tape Backup Drive	Lower drive cost	More expensive tapes, magnified with 20-tape rotation Slower speed Less capacity (10/20GB) Noise
DAT (DDS-4) Tape Backup Drive	Less expensive tapes, savings magnified with 20-tape rotation Faster speed Greater capacity (20/40GB) Virtually silent	More expensive drive cost

Table 6-1

For a 20-tape media rotation, after considering both the tape backup drive hardware and media costs, there's not much difference in cost between Travan and DAT backup solutions. However, DAT storage technology provides several compelling benefits.

Tip #80

Automate your backup system.

✓ **Save on Soft Costs**

Save on Out-of-Pocket Expenses

The goal of any backup system is ultimately to be a restore system. So the most crucial issue becomes, how can you ensure that your backup system will be ready when summoned for duty?

Getting the Job Done Right, at the Correct Time

At the most basic level, backup jobs need to be properly configured with the right settings *and* carried out consistently at predetermined times, generally daily.

The scheduling feature, from either your operating system or backup software application, can take care of this much-needed automation. Relying on manual steps always leads to trouble, either with procrastination, or more certainly the first time the designated backup system operator goes on vacation or is otherwise out of the office. Automated scheduling of backup jobs also removes the burden of remembering to launch the backup. In most cases, you'll want this automated backup routine to start after hours, when files are least likely to be in use.

Unattended Backup Software: Microsoft and Third-Party

In terms of software for unattended backup jobs, many versions of Microsoft Windows include backup software. With Microsoft Windows NT Workstation 4 and the Scheduled Task Wizard from Microsoft Internet Explorer 5, you can schedule unattended backup jobs through the Scheduled Task Wizard, reachable through the My Computer icon. With Microsoft Windows 2000 Professional, the scheduling mechanism is built right into the included Backup utility program, as seen in Figure 6-1.

Tip:
To learn more about the differences between consumer and business versions of Microsoft Windows, see Chapter 4.

Also, most third-party backup software programs, such as Computer Associates BrightStor ARCserve (www.ca.com) and VERITAS

Backup Exec (www.veritas.com), include intuitive scheduling tools to help automate your backup jobs.

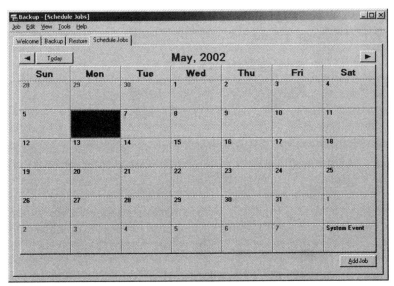

Figure 6-1

The Backup software included with Microsoft Windows 2000 Professional has an integrated scheduling function so backup jobs can be easily automated.

Planning for Adequate Storage Capacity

As you plan to automate your backup system, be sure your backup drive capacity is large enough so you don't have to swap out media in the middle of backup jobs. Automation loses much of its appeal when backup jobs must span more than one media unit or tape cartridge.

Because no one is likely to be around to change media at 2 a.m., be sure to select a backup system that is large enough, with ample room for growth, to back up all server volumes on a single media unit. There are backup systems with robotic mechanisms that automatically change media for you, but these are generally *way* beyond the price range a small business would budget for a robust backup system.

Tip #81

Test your backup system regularly and monitor its log files.

✓ **Save on Soft Costs**

Save on Out-of-Pocket Expenses

A backup system must be highly automated to ensure that jobs are launched consistently and correctly, but a backup system also needs to be watched over diligently to make sure it *continues* to function reliably. Unfortunately, monitoring the backup system generally isn't a priority until something goes wrong. By then it's too late.

People have a strong tendency with a backup system to set it and forget it. Automation clearly has many benefits, but a totally hands-off approach can be *very* dangerous if no one is overseeing the process.

Test and Then Test Again: *VERY* Important

With any newly installed backup system, don't assume everything works correctly right out of the box. Even more important, don't take for granted that your backup system will continue working indefinitely. You need periodically to restore some folders and files from your backup media to validate that your system still works.

If your automated backup routine is configured to include a verify run with each backup job, testing a sample restore job monthly should be adequate. However, if you have an extremely low tolerance for risk, you may want to simulate a sample restore job once a week.

Note:
A verify job compares the contents of what was just backed up to media against what resides on the hard drive.

The Hazard of Moving Parts and Open Design

Why do you need to take these precautions if you're purchasing a reliable, business-class backup system to start with? Typically, a tape drive or other backup device is one of the few components in a PC or server that still have moving parts.

As a result, it's prone to mechanical failure. In addition, because a backup device generally is open, as opposed to the sealed design of a hard drive, it's easy for the inside of the backup device to attract a significant dust buildup in a relatively short period of time.

Sample Restore Jobs and Cleaning Tape Heads

Testing a tape for a sample restore job is also a great time to clean the heads of the backup drive if your backup system requires this kind of maintenance.

Restoring a few hundred megabytes (MB) of data to a scratch directory and running a head-cleaning tape should take no more than 15 to 30 minutes.

When running a test restore job, always restore the data to an alternate server folder path, so as not to disrupt the use of any shared folders.

Tip:
If you use Microsoft Outlook, a personal information manager (PIM) or a similar scheduling program, you may want to set up a recurring monthly or weekly event in your calendar for testing the backup system and running your head-cleaning tape.

Building a Backup and Restore Procedure Checklist

In times of crisis, the most crucial issue becomes how quickly you can get the data back onto your system, undamaged.

So, as you build your backup system, be sure to document your test procedures into handy checklists.

This documentation also can be great for cross-training and crucial for avoiding panic during an emergency. Be sure you have a hard copy of this documentation next to your system *and* stored off-site with your backup media.

Watching the Log Files

In addition to running test restore jobs, you must inspect your backup system log files daily.

When the backup system is first installed, take time to get familiar with the way log files look when everything is working. This way, if something goes awry, you'll be better prepared to pinpoint the nature of the problem immediately.

As network operating system (NOS) suites and backup software have become more sophisticated, it's now possible to monitor backup system log files remotely and more proactively. In most cases, the backup system log files are just plain text (.txt) files.

185

Many third-party tools and utilities, as well as those included with Microsoft BackOffice Small Business Server (SBS) and Microsoft BackOffice Server, can automatically e-mail or fax a backup system log file at a preconfigured time.

Automatically and Remotely Monitoring Tape Backup Log Files

Many computer consultants have their small business clients' log files automatically e-mailed to them daily, so the consultants proactively can watch out for potential problems with the backup system.

However, don't think this proactive monitoring is limited to professional consultants. If your company has one or more branch offices you support from a centralized location, you also can use a similar method to monitor backup system health in remote locations.

For greater flexibility, you can set up an e-mail alias so the backup system log file automatically is sent to you, your second-in-command and perhaps an external computer consultant – so you are all kept in the loop. Also, this way, monitoring continues even when you're out of the office or on vacation.

Resource Directory:
Want an easy way to recall the over 60 Web site references discussed in this book? Check out the Resource Directory, starting on page 261, for suggested Web sites that deal with PC hardware and peripherals, software applications and operating systems, data protection and other general small business technology information.

Tip #82

Invest in a substantial media rotation plan and store backup media off-site.

✓ **Save on Soft Costs**

Save on Out-of-Pocket Expenses

In many cases, users won't notice that a file is missing or damaged until after a few days or even weeks have passed. So it's important to be able to roll back the state of files or folders several days if needed.

Case in Point

Our office uses a popular small business accounting program as a mission-critical application. My wife Jennifer, our publisher and business manager, handles most accounting functions on Mondays.

One Monday morning, Jennifer was in a temporary panic. As each check was posted, the accounting program choked out a Microsoft Windows Dr. Watson error. First, I tried restoring the data files from the previous day's backup, the previous Friday. As it turned out, the data already were corrupted by the previous Friday. So we tried rolling the accounting data back to the day before that, Thursday, but still got the same Dr. Watson errors when printing checks.

We finally had to roll back several days earlier to reach the last uncorrupted set of data, the previous Monday. Because the accounting program, at the time, was hardly ever used between Mondays, we didn't lose any data. But we did learn once again why it's crucial to have a lot more than three or five days' worth of full system backups on hand. It was a classic case of the media rotation's saving the day.

Media Rotation Strategy

For most small businesses, I recommend purchasing 32 media units (i.e. tapes) to get you through the first year. Yes, this expense can add up, but it's generally *extremely* trivial compared to the value of your company's information that the media is protecting.

Twenty of the media should be allocated to your four-week rotation, as shown in Table 6-2. The remaining 12 media are for permanent monthly archives. Required in many industries and recommended for all, a permanent monthly archive should be created at the same time each month and then immediately labeled, write protected and stored off-site. Be sure also to label each backup media unit clearly with server name, week number and day of week, or month and year.

Sample Weekly and Monthly Media Rotation Plan

Week A	Mon A	Tue A	Wed A	Thu A	Fri A	
Week B	Mon B	Tue B	Wed B	Thu B	Fri B	
Week C	Mon C	Tue C	Wed C	Thu C	Fri C	
Week D	Mon D	Tue D	Wed D	Thu D	Fri D	
Permanent Archive	Jan	Feb	Mar	Apr	May	Jun
	Jul	Aug	Sep	Oct	Nov	Dec

Table 6-2

Because data corruption or data loss isn't always that obvious, I recommend investing in a four-week daily backup media rotation, as well as one year's worth of permanent archive media.

Off-Site Media Rotation

Now that your media rotation is in place, plan your off-site rotation. This can be as simple as having the company owner, office manager or internal guru take the backup media home daily or once a week. Be sure the off-site location is physically secure and readily accessible. Some companies use a bank safe-deposit box for this. Other businesses with multiple locations send backup media back and forth among locations for off-site storage.

In most cases, rotating media off-site weekly works just fine, unless your company cannot afford to lose a week's worth of data. There's nothing particularly high-tech here. But if your office gets flooded, burned down or broken into, it won't do you much good if your backup media were sitting on top of your PC or server.

Many small business owners resist sending backup media off-site, insisting that the media are secure in the company's fireproof safe. This sounds good in theory, but even a fireproof safe may not protect the data on the media adequately. During a fire, the media superficially will appear to be physically unharmed, but the *data* on the media, however, can often be damaged beyond recognition.

Tip #83

Create permanent archives and retire backup media *before* degradation.

✓ **Save on Soft Costs**

Save on Out-of-Pocket Expenses

As we just saw, most small businesses can derive tremendous benefits from taking a permanent snapshot backup of the way their system looks at the same time each month. This is one of those cases when borrowing best practices from Fortune 1000 IT really makes sense.

I advise running a permanent archive backup once a month. If it's easier to keep track of this task, you may want to create your monthly permanent archive tape on the same day you run a test restore job, as discussed earlier in this chapter.

Because It Sometimes Takes a While to Notice Something's Missing

For projects you may not touch for four weeks, things that may only be done monthly, quarterly or annually, you may not realize that files or folders are missing from your system or have been corrupted for quite some time. However, by investing in an extra archive backup once a month, you'll be able to go back in time to find missing files or folders. At least two or three times a year, I retrieve a permanent archive and I count my blessings that we had the persistence to stick with this simple, relatively inexpensive, data protection regimen.

In terms of implementing the extra permanent archive backup into your four-week rotation, I've seen small businesses take all sorts of approaches. Most have had great success with replacing Friday A or Friday D with permanent archive media. This way, the previous days' media go off-site with the permanent archive media, which gets write protected and simply stays off-site indefinitely.

Tip:
In most cases, you can write protect backup media by simply sliding the notch over on top of the write protect area. This is very similar to the write protect tab you already may be familiar with on 3.5-inch diskettes.

What To Do at the End of the First Year

At the end of your first year of the 32-tape backup system, you'll be left with the 20 tapes in the four-week rotation.

At that point, you should begin to gradually retire media from the rotation.

In much the same way standard audiocassette tapes wear out, backup media become less reliable as they age.

You don't want to wait until the media become worthless before making the retirement decision.

Glossary:
Have you visited this book's Glossary yet? Get a quick refresher on over 160 terms used throughout this book – all those buzzwords and acronyms frequently thrown around by computer consultants and other techies. The Glossary, with extensive cross-references and chapter references, begins on page 231.

I generally advise small businesses to retire media after they've been used anywhere from 12 to 24 times. So, at the beginning of year two, purchase an additional 20 media units for your four-week rotation and retire the previous year's media units.

The previous year's 20 media units then will get one final workout as permanent monthly archive tapes for the next year and eight months.

You should repeat this replace-and-retire rotation annually to ensure that your backup media remain fresh and reliable.

Also, create and retain permanent monthly archive media *indefinitely* using the recycled media for year two and beyond.

Tip:
Some companies selectively archive data on CD-R media. However, because of the storage space limitations of roughly 600MB to 700MB of data, CD-R media only work well as permanent archives in limited situations, if your company has an *extremely* small set of data files.

Tip #84

Factor in special software application needs, as well as unprotected data on individual PCs, notebooks and handhelds.

✓ **Save on Soft Costs**

Save on Out-of-Pocket Expenses

When planning your backup system, consider software applications with special backup requirements. Although any application that requires certain files to be open constantly is a potential problem, some *very* popular server-based applications must be considered at all times.

Potential Pitfalls in Backing Up E-mail and Database Servers

Make sure your backup software accommodates various specialty applications. For example, popular small business LAN-based applications such as Microsoft Exchange Server and Microsoft SQL Server have unique data backup needs.

One of the major selling points of third-party tape backup software is its ability to truncate transaction logs for Microsoft Exchange Server and Microsoft SQL Server. So make sure any creatively assembled, homegrown, backup methods take this crucial concern into account.

Multi-Server Backup Issues

When considering unusual backup requirements, also consider whether all server data are on one server or dispersed on two or more.

In most cases, third-party backup software is available in both single- and multi-server licenses. So if you depend on data on more than one server, be sure your backup software can handle that requirement.

Backing Up Files That Never Close

Also pay attention to any open files, such as those that are *always* in use, that show up in the backup log files. If your backup system doesn't back up open files, make sure your users are aware of this limitation so they can close data files on their network drives each day.

You even can show some power users how to check Windows Explorer for the presence of the Archive bit (A) to see whether their files have been backed up. In Figure 6-2, you can tell that the Microsoft

Word and Microsoft Excel data files have *not* yet been backed up because the Archive bit (A) in the Attributes column is still enabled. After the files have been backed up through a normal or full backup, the Archive bit would be cleared from the Attributes column.

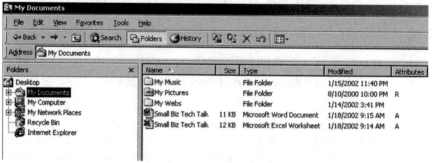

Figure 6-2

You can train power users to check for the presence of the Archive bit (A) in the Attributes column of Windows Explorer. This way, your power users will be able to tell whether their files are being backed up.

Tip:
In Microsoft Windows 2000 Professional, if you do not see the Attributes column in Windows Explorer, you can enable the Attributes field through the View, Choose Columns command.

The Hazards of Decentralized Data Storage

In addition to unusual backup software requirements, watch out for unprotected data that may be residing on individual end users' PCs, notebooks and handheld personal digital assistants (PDAs).

Note:
For details on PDA data storage issues, see Tip #41 in Chapter 2.

If your backup system is only configured to back up files stored on your server or servers, be sure your end users and their managers are aware that any files stored on *local* hard drives of desktop PCs or notebooks won't be backed up automatically. Be especially alert for any end user mailbox files, such as Microsoft Outlook Personal Folders Files (.pst) and Microsoft Internet Explorer Favorites folders, which may be stored on users' local hard drives and not automatically backed up.

Tip #85

Physically secure your backup system and media.

✓ **Save on Soft Costs**

Save on Out-of-Pocket Expenses

Your backup media are a very compact and portable form of your company's intellectual property. Guard them accordingly.

Dangerous Vulnerabilities

No matter how much time and resources you invest in creating a secure network and technology backbone, your backup media ultimately may be your weakest link.

For example, if your server is not locked up and someone has access to your office after hours, removing backup media could be as simple as pressing the eject button on the front of the backup drive.

If these backup media contain your company's entire set of data and intellectual property *and* can fit in a shirt pocket and go undetected right out of the building, this dramatically underscores the need to make physical security a *very* high priority.

Media and Your Company Walking Out the Door

For the same reasons, even your backup media need to be physically secured. It does no good to keep the server in a locked room if you keep backup media in plain sight on a desk, or in an unsecured desk drawer or file cabinet.

I'm always amazed by the great lengths small businesses will go to lock up a few hundred dollars of petty cash, but give little or no thought to potentially millions of dollars of unprotected information assets.

Controlling Your Media Assets

To help physically control media, media rotations, and the outcome of various backup and restore jobs, I suggest setting up a logbook to track the disposition of your backup system media.

At the minimum, the log should indicate the media label (i.e. Wednesday C), the date the media were last used for a backup, the date the media left for the off-site location and the date the media returned from the off-site location.

Someone other than the person responsible for the included tasks should audit this log regularly.

Figure 6-3 shows a sample Tape Backup Log Book Template.

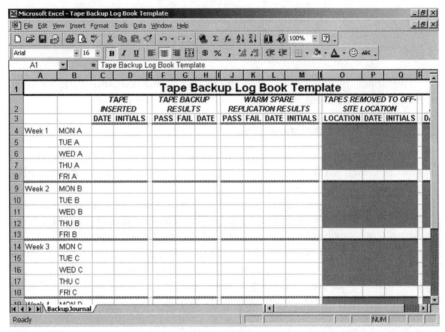

Figure 6-3

Because your backup media include so much of your company's data and intellectual property, you must keep track of the media's whereabouts. A logbook can be a great way for your company to manage these information assets.

Table of Tips:
Need a quick refresher on the 101 money-saving tips discussed in this book? Check out the Table of Tips, beginning on page 267, for a chapter-by-chapter recap and quick reference.

Tip #86

Know the pros and cons of online Internet backup services.

✓ **Save on Soft Costs**

✓ **Save on Out-of-Pocket Expenses**

In Chapter 5, we discussed the concept of rentable software as a service, otherwise known as the Application Service Provider (ASP) business model, and why renting software is *very* risky, as the majority of the ASP industry is in uncertain financial health.

Same Security and Internet Access Challenges as ASP-Based Software Solutions

In addition, we saw how many small businesses aren't able to get affordable, reliable, high-speed Internet access, a big prerequisite for a successful experience with a rented software application. We also discussed small business owners' natural reluctance to allow third-party control over proprietary data.

Many technology companies, straddling the line between ASPs and traditional Web-hosting Internet Service Providers (ISPs), have offered online backup capabilities to supplement more conventional tape backup methods.

Benefits and Risks

Aside from not needing to invest in backup system hardware or media, online Internet backup services promote how your data go off-site immediately. There's no waiting for someone to take media off-site to a remote location and no waiting for retrieval of those media when you need to restore data.

Online Internet backup providers insist that they have adequate security controls to ensure that the data you entrust to them are safe. However, for largely the same reasons the ASP model of renting software is not quite functional, I recommend that most small businesses proceed *extremely* cautiously with any online Internet backup service. With all the dot-com business failures and security breaches in the past year or two, I don't see much peace of mind in contracting for online Internet backup services.

Tip #87

Configure a low-budget data replication system.

✓ **Save on Soft Costs**

✓ **Save on Out-of-Pocket Expenses**

Fortune 1000 IT departments almost always have some kind of real time, or semi-real time, routine for replicating files and folders from one server to another. In many cases, for disaster recovery planning, this replication occurs over a wide area network (WAN) link. This way there is a duplicate of crucial files in another geographic location.

World Class Best Practices on a Small Business Budget

Many small businesses mistakenly assume that this kind of replication is beyond their budgetary reach. However, even without a WAN or high-speed Internet access connection, you should be able to replicate key server folders to another server at least once a day -- even if that second server is only another physically secured, high-end desktop PC with a large hard drive in another part of the building.

Using the highly intuitive Scheduled Task Wizard, you can create a simple batch file that copies folders from one mapped drive to another, unattended. Even without a second server class machine, or one running a network operating system, you still can achieve a certain degree of fault tolerance.

The Backup to the Tape Backup Drive

Because your backup system hardware is one of the few items in a server with moving parts, the backup system is often the least reliable component in any server. Many small businesses only have one server, so you can use the Scheduled Task Wizard to copy workgroup shared folders and user shared folders overnight to a physically secured PC. For extra protection, this PC should use the more secure NTFS file system included with business versions of Microsoft Windows.

Not only does this method provide a backup for the backup system hardware, the target desktop PC even could provide limited file and printer sharing services temporarily, with up to 10 simultaneous connections, if the server went down for whatever reason. Just be sure to factor this target system into your enhanced physical security plans.

The Bottom Line

A good data backup system is a lot like an insurance policy -- you hope you never need to put in a claim, but you sleep a *lot* better knowing your company is covered. However, much like insurance policies, not all small business backup systems are created equal.

Many of the seemingly low-cost backup systems available are either unreliable, slow, labor-intensive or get *very* expensive as the amount of required backup media increases. But choosing, implementing, testing and maintaining the right kind of backup system often can be the difference between survival and failure during any data disaster.

Take time to plan carefully your company's backup system. Consider automation, testing and monitoring needs, as well as various media planning such as daily and weekly tape rotations, off-site storage and permanent monthly archives.

In addition, make sure you consider *all* sources of valuable company information in your backup plan, including specialty applications and data stored on desktop PCs, notebooks and personal digital assistants (PDAs).

Finally, don't neglect physical security. A backup system is a *very* important part of your company's overall technology infrastructure. However, you'll lose much of your competitive advantage if a sleazy competitor is able to send someone in after hours to lift a tape backup cartridge sitting out in a visible area of your company's office.

Resource Box

- **Computer Associates** -- www.ca.com

- **Hewlett Packard** -- www.hp.com

- **IDC** -- www.idc.com

- **Joshua Feinberg's Small Biz Tech Talk** -- www.smallbiztechtalk.com

- **Seagate Technology** -- www.seagate.com

- **VERITAS** -- www.veritas.com

Companion CD-ROM

Are you ready to take your cost-savings to the next level, but you're at a loss for the *right* questions to ask? Check out the Companion CD-ROM for *What Your Computer Consultant Doesn't Want You to Know* -- with over 550 Action Items to get you started saving money right now.

The Action Items are presented in a variety of convenient file formats including Adobe Acrobat .pdf, HTML, Microsoft Word .doc and Microsoft Excel .xls. In addition, the Action Items are loaded up in a Microsoft Outlook Personal Folders File (.pst) -- ready for you to import into your Microsoft Outlook Tasks. The Companion CD-ROM also includes an electronic Resource Directory, recapping the book's suggested Web sites, that's all set for you to import into your Microsoft Internet Explorer Favorites list. Use the handy Action Item format to copy, paste and delegate -- while you tailor the money-saving program to your company's unique needs.

For more information on the Companion CD-ROM, see page 285.

Or visit www.smallbiztechtalk.com/tools/ to download sample Action Items or order the Companion CD-ROM.

Chapter 7
Power Protection

Product Selection, Scope of Coverage,
Proactive Planning, Testing, Monitoring
and Early Warning Signs

Are your computers ready to weather the strain of brownouts, blackouts, surges and sags? If you answered "Not Sure" or "No," you're certainly not alone. In most small businesses, unless you have an in-house computer support person, or a similar arrangement with a local consultant, your computers, phone system and telecommunications equipment may be a *lot* more vulnerable than you realize. Unfortunately, when it comes to all things related to data protection, vulnerability means exposure to *huge* potential expenses.

Although power disturbances can take on many forms, the most common root cause is the fact that utility companies cannot provide electrical power consistently *and* cleanly enough for various computer hardware devices. So your company needs a strategy for coping with this lack of power reliability. You need to protect not only your hardware from physical damage like getting fried, but even more important, your irreplaceable company data.

I find that a lot of small business managers feel impervious to power problems. My response, "I see you have eight software applications open on your PC right now and 14 people connected to the server. What would happen if I yanked the power cord out of the wall *right now* without warning you to first save your files?"

If I were to try this in an office without a battery backup unit, I'd likely get escorted to the door *very* fast. But, this example does drive the message home. Chapter 7 is all about layering your defenses to cope with common utility power-induced data threats.

Tip #88

Make sure you purchase the right power protection products.

✓ **Save on Soft Costs**

Save on Out-of-Pocket Expenses

Many power protection products for small businesses are available, but there are two main tools that *must* be in your power protection arsenal: surge protectors and battery backup units.

Tip:
A battery backup unit is basically synonymous with an uninterruptible power supply (UPS). A surge protector is roughly the same as a surge suppressor.

Surge Protectors

Relative Cost Indicator: $

A surge protector, which defends your hardware from damaging power fluctuations, should not be confused with a mere power strip, which only gives you more electric receptacles and *no* power protection. Ever year I hear sad accounts from hundreds of small business owners who thought they had surge protectors, but merely had virtually *worthless* power strips. Don't be fooled by power strips in the $5 to $10 price range. Expect to spend a minimum of $15 to $35 for a business grade surge suppressor from one of the leading manufacturers of power protection devices.

I've always been very happy with the reliability, variety and value of APC's (www.apcc.com) power protection products. However, Tripp Lite (www.tripplite.com) is also a very popular power protection vendor among small businesses and technology professionals.

Most business-grade surge suppressors, and virtually all UPS units, include equipment protection warranties -- the ethical equivalent of the vendor's money where its mouth is. If you do not see any financial guarantee on the product packaging, keep looking for another surge protector or UPS unit. For example, the APC Personal SurgeArrest currently includes a $2,500 lifetime equipment protection policy. Basic business-grade surge protectors also typically include a "Protection working indicator," distinct from a more generic, ambiguous "Power" LED indicator.

Battery Backup Units

Relative Cost Indicator: $-$$-$$$

If you've ever heard the horrible screaming sound a person makes when his or her PC crashes or loses power suddenly, with a half-dozen applications running and hours of not-yet-saved data, you'll understand why a UPS unit is mandatory for any office with valuable information on PC or server hard drives.

UPS units run the gamut. There are very basic, entry-level units, in the $100 to $200 price range, perfect for your desktop PCs, as well as mid-range units generally priced between $400 and $800, designed for small file servers. In addition, there's a whole separate category of high-end UPS products, with hours of runtime, optimized for corporate data centers.

A UPS unit goes one *crucial* step beyond the protection afforded by a surge protector. A UPS protects your *data* from improper termination by providing several minutes of battery backup power -- allowing you to save your work, close open files and shut Microsoft Windows gracefully *before* power is lost. Thus, a UPS protects your data files, operating system files, software application files and all the related configuration settings.

Because the feature set and run-time capacity of UPS units *vary* considerably among models, you'll need to use vendor-supplied sizing tools *before* making your purchase selection. These sizing tools will help you pick UPS units capable of handling your unique combinations of operating systems, software applications, computer system units, monitors and related peripherals.

Selecting the Right UPS

Most leading manufacturers of power protection products now include sizing tools on their Web sites. For example, APC's UPS Selector is a free online tool (www.apcc.com/template/size/apc/) shown in Figure 7-1 that helps you choose a battery backup unit for individual PCs, servers, storage peripherals and telecommunications equipment.

To compensate for fluctuations in utility power, a UPS unit constantly monitors your line voltage and trims back on power overages accordingly. At the same time, a UPS unit can boost power as needed to compensate for any power sags.

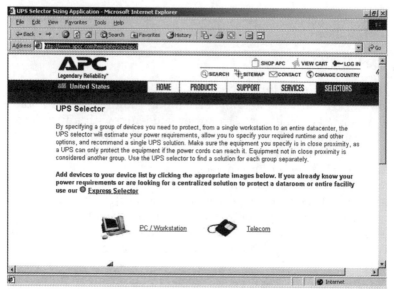

Figure 7-1

The APC UPS Selector is a free, interactive online tool that helps you decide on the right battery backup unit for your unique requirements.

Because these changes in utility voltage are often incredibly fast, the battery backup unit must be able to switch over to battery power *extremely* fast to avoid data loss. In fact, one of the major differentiators between an entry-level UPS unit and a more advanced, server-grade, battery backup unit is the transfer time between utility power and battery. There are also much more expensive online UPS units that maintain a constant live connection with the battery backup power source, virtually eliminating transfer time.

Unattended Shutdown Capability

A server-grade battery backup unit absolutely needs to have unattended shutdown capability. Through a hardware interface, typically implemented through either the serial or USB port, the battery backup unit is in constant real-time communication with the power management software running on the server.

Tip:
Many inexpensive, entry-level, desktop UPS units include an interface to the PC for limited power management functions and unattended shutdown capabilities. This is a great feature I strongly recommend.

Unattended shutdown capability, working hand in hand with the operating system, is designed to kick in when the server has been on battery for a preconfigured amount of time. Because servers usually are running 7-by-24 and small businesses *rarely* have around-the-clock on-site computer support, the battery backup unit needs to be able to shut the server down *gracefully* when no one is available to perform the shutdown task manually. Note that this *graceful,* automated shutdown is vitally important to preventing data corruption and data loss associated with hard crash shutdowns.

Because the UPS interface and its included power management software need to communicate properly with your PC or server hardware, operating system and software applications, it's very important to ask about interface and operating system compatibility, *before* you buy. The power management software needs to be compatible and preferably vendor-certified for your desired operating system. Also be sure you have an available serial or USB port on your PC or server.

Other Power Protection Products

Relative Cost Indicator: $$-$$$-$$$$

Depending on the amount of battery backup power you need, as measured in minutes or hours, a battery backup unit may not be the only or best solution. You may need a generator as well. If you require several minutes, or up to a few hours, a UPS unit may be adequate. However, if you require backup power for potentially several hours or several days, consider investing in a generator to supplement your battery backup unit.

In addition, if your power source is *extremely* unreliable, you may need to supplement your surge protectors and UPS units with a line conditioner. Leading power protection product vendors, such as APC, offer line conditioners, also known as power conditioners or automatic voltage regulators.

Installing and safely transporting a UPS

When you first unpack a new UPS, the first thing you'll likely need to do is reconnect the ground wire. Each UPS product is just a little different, so be sure to follow the manufacturer's instructions and illustrations included in the box. UPS manufacturers disconnect the ground wire during shipment, for safety reasons.

If you need to return the UPS to the manufacturer for warranty service, or to ship the unit to another location, be sure to disconnect the ground wire *before* repackaging the unit.

Tip #89

Install comprehensive power protection on *every* sensitive electronic device.

✓ **Save on Soft Costs**

Save on Out-of-Pocket Expenses

Make sure *every* piece of sensitive electronic equipment in your office has some form of surge suppression. Although most people intuitively think of their PCs and monitors first, it's just as important to factor in external modems, hubs, routers, switches, workgroup laser printers, telephones, cell phone chargers and fax machines.

Data Line Protection for Modems and Phones

Also, don't overlook data line power protection. Besides surges and spikes coming in from electric utility receptacles, surges and spikes also can originate from telecommunication lines. Power surges and spikes can go right from telephone and cable-TV circuits to your modem or network card, and literally fry the innards of your PC -- causing some *very* expensive damage.

So be sure your surge protector has data line protection, or simply purchase a stand-alone data line surge protector separately to sit between your telecommunication circuits and equipment. Also, make sure you read the included instructions and actually use the data line protection device properly. For stand-alone data line surge protectors, the product generally needs to be grounded to be effective.

Protecting High-Speed Data Circuits

Also don't overlook the many data circuits you may have coming into your office, beyond basic analog telephone lines. To be well-protected, consider installing data line protection for any advanced telecommunication circuits in your office such as ISDN, xDSL, Frame Relay, Fractional T1/T3 and cable modem.

Protecting Modems in Notebook PCs

And a few crucial words about notebook power protection for the road warriors among us: Most top power protection vendors make inexpensive, portable surge protectors, with data line protection, especially for notebooks.

Tip #90

Isolate your hardware assets from power dominating appliances, overloaded circuits and human error.

✓ **Save on Soft Costs**

Save on Out-of-Pocket Expenses

Obviously, some power disturbances are beyond your control, but many *can* be prevented. And that's what this chapter is all about!

Overloaded Outlets and Circuits

For example, in many offices I often see outlets overloaded with surge protectors, piggybacked onto more surge protectors. Not only is this practice a potential fire hazard, it diminishes the effectiveness of the surge protection. If you find *any* evidence of surge protectors daisy-chained to other surge protectors, fix the problem immediately -- ask questions later.

Also, UPS units *always* should be plugged directly into your electrical wall receptacles. A UPS unit *never* should be daisy-chained to another UPS unit, surge protector or vice versa. Place all surge protectors and UPS units directly into properly grounded, three-pronged outlets, or their equivalent outside of the U.S.

By figuring out which outlets are on which circuits, you also can improve *dramatically* your system reliability. For example, if a single outlet is on a dedicated 20-amp circuit, commonly referred to by electricians as a home run, that single outlet can provide *much* cleaner power than if six outlets are on that same 20-amp circuit.

In the field, I often see power-monopolizing appliances, such as photocopy machines, microwave ovens, space heaters and window-unit air conditioners, plugged into the same circuit as sensitive electronic equipment. If you value your data and equipment, this is a *huge* blunder.

If you have *any* doubts about the condition of your office's electrical wiring, hire a licensed electrician to do an inspection of your circuits, and perhaps set up a dedicated circuit for your server and related network peripherals.

Remember, a battery backup unit can go only so far. If your electrical wiring is a total mess, you'll have a very difficult time ever achieving superior network reliability.

Kiddy Plugs as Power Protection Saviors

If you have young children at home, you probably have placed plastic kiddy plugs over open receptacles. Kiddy plugs cover up exposed receptacles and help to deter dangerous childhood experiments.

Also consider kiddy plugs to help with staff and contractors who need to plug in various appliances from time and time, and in haste plug their drill or vacuum cleaner into the first available outlet.

I began recommending plugging open outlets on surge protectors and UPS units with kiddy plugs several years ago when one of my clients kept breaking UPS units as employees plugged in space heaters.

This client had more expensive frustration when the overnight cleaning crew began plugging industrial vacuum cleaners and tile-waxing machines into UPS units.

Homemade fluorescent warning labels and $2 worth of plastic kiddy plugs from the local hardware store quickly and inexpensively solved the problem. (Figure 7-2)

Figure 7-2

Inexpensive kiddy plugs and homemade WARNING labels can provide a gentle reminder to avoid plugging power-monopolizing appliances into surge protectors and UPS units.

The Dangers of Wall Switches

Second, and this tip may be obvious only *after* you've been caught short, don't plug surge protectors or UPS units into receptacles that are controlled by wall switches. (Figure 7-3)

Resource Directory:
Want an easy way to recall the over 60 Web site references discussed in this book? Check out the Resource Directory, starting on page 261, for suggested Web sites that deal with PC hardware and peripherals, software applications and operating systems, data protection and other general small business technology information.

I've seen the wall switch problem all too often. A client was getting ready to celebrate its office manager's birthday, with a cake, candles and a few rounds of "Happy Birthday" from coworkers.

To dim the lights, someone turned off an electrical switch that immediately sent the server's UPS unit into battery backup mode. Fortunately, the client had installed UPS units, which prevented a nightmare. Within a few minutes of devouring the delicious birthday cake, we were relocating the server UPS unit to a *non*-switched receptacle and circuit.

Figure 7-3

Make sure your sensitive computer equipment is not plugged into power receptacles controlled by wall switches.

Free E-mail Newsletter:
Would you like a convenient way to keep up with new tips and techniques from Small Biz Tech Talk? Take control of your technology now! Subscribe to the free bi-weekly Tips newsletter at www.smallbiztechtalk.com

Tip #91

Test your battery backup units regularly and watch the UPS log file for clues.

✓ **Save on Soft Costs**

Save on Out-of-Pocket Expenses

As does your tape backup system, UPS units and their accompanying software and interfaces need to be tested, to ensure that no unpleasant surprises occur at inopportune times.

Although most popular power management software applications included with battery backup units have several built-in self-test mechanisms, the *best* test is one that approximates the real life usage of a power failure, as in a sudden blackout.

Testing, Testing, 1-2-3

When testing your UPS units, be sure no users are logged onto the protected system and that there are no related open files. Therefore, this testing often is best accomplished after hours.

To test the battery backup unit, pull the UPS unit power cord out of the electric receptacle and see what happens.

As a more conservative test, if you wish to preserve the grounding, turn off the electrical circuit at your power box in your utility closet.

Before you do this, make sure you've considered the effect on any other items that are plugged into this circuit. For example, if your office's alarm system happens to be on this circuit, will tripping the power cause a false alarm?

UPS Software

When a server-grade UPS unit switches to battery power, the UPS unit should be signaling its related power management software to send out an alert message to PCs on the network. These popup messages will advise users on your LAN that the UPS is on battery, while displaying a countdown of how many minutes remain before the server UPS shuts the server down automatically.

However, because you've presumably already told your users the network will be down for testing, you'll likely only want one or two PCs booted up and logged on for monitoring purposes. Be sure to have one or two PCs logged onto the network, so you can confirm whether the alerting capability is working properly.

Many utility power disturbances are relatively brief. So normal utility power is restored *before* the battery backup unit initiates its automated server shutdown sequence. When this happens, PCs on the network should be notified that normal power has been restored.

Log File Clues

Server-grade UPS units with power management software usually also include detailed logging capability, which can be an *extremely* effective diagnostic tool. A regularly occurring event in this log file often can lead to solving an evasive, nagging power problem.

In one case I recall, a unique overvoltage occurred on Saturdays and Sundays at exactly 2 a.m. After doing some detective work, the client and I discovered that there was an air-conditioning unit programmed to start up at that time on weekends. We also found out in the process that the electrician had *not* properly wired a dedicated circuit, as requested, for the server.

The UPS communications interface, via USB or serial port, provides these advanced functions such as unattended shutdowns of your computer during extended blackouts, scheduled self-testing, as well as the logging of the time, date, duration and magnitude of a power fluctuation.

To get a pulse on just how good or bad your utility power is, be sure to review regularly your UPS log files in the days immediately after installation, and periodically thereafter.

Glossary:
Have you visited this book's Glossary yet? Get a quick refresher on over 160 terms used throughout this book -- all those buzzwords and acronyms frequently thrown around by computer consultants and other techies. The Glossary, with extensive cross-references and chapter references, begins on page 231.

Tip #92

Learn to recognize the early warning signs of power problems.

✓ **Save on Soft Costs**

Save on Out-of-Pocket Expenses

In much the same way a small business office manager should be able to detect the early warning signs of incipient personnel problems, a small business internal computer administrator needs to know enough about power protection to be capable of sensing that something is wrong.

Until now, this chapter has given you the background to properly purchase, install and maintain many power protection devices. Besides these previously discussed items, here are a few other factors that can be frequent harbingers of bigger power problems.

Self-Tests

A self-test generally is run automatically when you first turn on a UPS unit, and then at recurring, prescheduled intervals. If the initial power-on self-test or recurring scheduled self-test fails, you immediately should contact the UPS vendor and seek a replacement unit.

This sort of failure should be regarded with the same urgency and severity as you would a failed power-on self-test on a PC or server.

In addition, if you have a UPS that logs events using power management software, you also should be able to determine the date and time of the last successful self-test.

Note:

Because a UPS typically runs the self-test when you first turn the unit on, you generally want to wait to power on any devices plugged into the UPS until *after* the self-test is complete. As a result, avoid using the on/off switch on your UPS unit to simultaneously turn on or turn off all of the plugged-in hardware devices.

Lights and Beeps

In addition to gauges in the included power management software, nearly all UPS units include a unique assortment of beeps and LED indicators that tell you the status of a UPS unit's health or lack thereof.

Because these audible and visual alarms vary by manufacturer and model, be sure to read through the first few pages of any included product documentation and get familiar with the good and bad indicators.

If your UPS unit chronically switches to battery backup power, such as several times a day *every* day, this may indicate a bigger electrical problem in the building.

As with anything electrical-related in this chapter, if your gut instinct tells you it's a power problem, get a licensed electrician in to check things out fast! Think of a UPS unit's diagnostic power as something like a doctor's stethoscope -- it has an uncanny ability to give you a true pulse on underlying electrical problems.

Site Wiring Faults

Most UPS units and even many business-grade surge protectors also include a site wiring fault indicator, sometimes referred to as a building wiring fault indicator. This LED will illuminate when there are grounding problems with building wiring, which can result in hardware damage and lead to a shock hazard.

Ask your electrician to inspect wiring for one or more of these conditions: overloaded neutral, reverse polarity or a missing group wire.

In addition to site wiring fault indicators on UPS units and surge protectors, you can purchase an inexpensive outlet tester, such as the one shown in Figure 7-4, at local hardware stores for less than $10. These outlet testers generally have two or three lights that, with the help of an included legend, will give you an immediate read on the status of an electrical receptacle.

Table of Tips:
Need a quick refresher on the 101 money-saving tips discussed in this book? Check out the Table of Tips, beginning on page 267, for a chapter-by-chapter recap and quick reference.

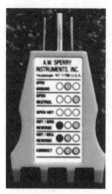

Figure 7-4

An inexpensive outlet tester can help you diagnose whether a U.S. three-pronged outlet is wired correctly. Many surge protectors and battery backup units have a built-in LED indicator that performs a subset of these ground-fault-wiring testing functions.

Running on Empty

Almost all UPS units include a low battery indicator, also sometimes called a replace battery indicator. The name is so self-describing, I won't bore you with the details. But I will say that, when you see such a light illuminated, you are on *borrowed* time, in much the same way you might see an ominous Check Engine Light on the dashboard of your car.

The UPS unit probably still will be very reliable as a surge protector even with a weakened battery, but you should contact your UPS vendor ASAP to order a replacement battery.

With most small business-sized UPS units, you should have no problem replacing the battery cartridge on your own. In fact, the procedure is very similar to the one you did earlier in this chapter when you connected the ground wire.

Finally, *never* try to force a three-pronged surge suppressor or UPS unit power cord into a two-pronged outlet.

The Bottom Line

Just as we saw with data backup in Chapter 6, by the time you know you have a *major* power problem, it's too late to do anything about it. However, because unreliable utility power has such a *huge* potential to damage your company's information and hardware assets, it's crucial to take proactive measures now. Comprehensive small business power protection begins by ensuring that you've purchased the right products, while exercising equal care to cover all bases within your organization.

And as with most hazards related to data protection, you never finish taking care of power protection – it's an ongoing process. You constantly need to be alert for possible employee errors and faulty electrical wiring, with the potential to sabotage your best efforts.

In addition, your power protection procedures should include regular testing and monitoring of key devices and software, as well as developing a keen sense for related, underlying power problems.

By putting the tips in this chapter to work, you'll go a long way toward preventing *extremely* expensive dangers to your company's equipment, data, productivity and business continuity.

Resource Box

- **APC (American Power Conversion)** --
  www.apcc.com

- **APC UPS Selector** --
  www.apcc.com/template/size/apc/

- **Joshua Feinberg's Small Biz Tech Talk** --
  www.smallbiztechtalk.com

- **Tripp Lite** -- www.tripplite.com

Companion CD-ROM

Are you ready to take your cost-savings to the next level, but you're at a loss for the *right* questions to ask? Check out the Companion CD-ROM for *What Your Computer Consultant Doesn't Want You to Know* -- with over 550 Action Items to get you started saving money right now.

The Action Items are presented in a variety of convenient file formats including Adobe Acrobat .pdf, HTML, Microsoft Word .doc and Microsoft Excel .xls. In addition, the Action Items are loaded up in a Microsoft Outlook Personal Folders File (.pst) -- ready for you to import into your Microsoft Outlook Tasks. The Companion CD-ROM also includes an electronic Resource Directory, recapping the book's suggested Web sites, that's all set for you to import into your Microsoft Internet Explorer Favorites list. Use the handy Action Item format to copy, paste and delegate -- while you tailor the money-saving program to your company's unique needs.

For more information on the Companion CD-ROM, see page 285.

Or visit www.smallbiztechtalk.com/tools/ to download sample Action Items or order the Companion CD-ROM.

Chapter 8
Virus Protection

*Defending the Whole Network, Media Rotation,
Internet-Era Threats, Forcing Manual Updates,
Maintaining the Engine and Definitions,
Proactive User Training and Hoaxes*

In Chapter 6, we discussed the ways a sound backup system protects your company from data loss and potentially exorbitant emergency computer support expenses. Then, in Chapter 7, we saw how various power protection devices guard against everything from expensive hardware damage and data corruption to catastrophic data loss.

Now, in the concluding chapter of Part III on Data Protection, we'll survey some cost-effective, easy-to-implement ways to shield your small business from computer viruses -- and their devastating data loss impact and time-consuming clean-up costs.

Ten years ago, it was difficult to get a virus through anything but infected diskettes. Now it's a lot easier to become a victim. Highly destructive and rapidly propagating viruses can infect your hard drive through e-mail programs, Web browsers and other Internet-borne mechanisms. In fact, today's viruses and security vulnerabilities make the primitive pre-Internet-era viruses seem utterly inconsequential.

This chapter will help you get proactive about virus protection and take steps to avoid the bothersome expenses associated with virus infiltration, infection and data contamination.

Tip #93

Purchase and install antivirus software for *all* your desktop PCs, notebooks and servers.

✓ **Save on Soft Costs**

✓ **Save on Out-of-Pocket Expenses**

Effective virus protection begins by inventorying the brand and version of antivirus software running on your company's desktop PCs, notebooks and servers. After all, you can correct deficiencies only when you pinpoint their existence.

Taking Inventory of Your Antivirus Software

A small business doesn't need to invest in expensive asset management software for compiling a software inventory. A visit to each PC and a simple Microsoft Excel workbook will suffice. If you as yet don't have a worksheet for tracking some aspect of your PC asset inventory, now's a great time to create one.

Suggested column headings for tackling an antivirus software inventory include

- Computer Name

- Operating System Version

- Antivirus Software Program (Vendor, Product Name, Version Number)

- Date of Last Update

Antivirus Software Bundled with Your PC Purchase

You should own a valid antivirus software license for each supported system. Be especially wary of any PCs that may have come bundled with preinstalled antivirus software. In many cases, these bundled offerings are introductory licenses that expire 90 days after the PC purchase date.

If your company has more than a few systems, you may find it more cost-effective and easier to manage if you consolidate all of your antivirus software purchases into an annual or biannual site license.

Alternatively, you could purchase a stand-alone retail copy of anti-virus software, and a related update subscription, for each of your company's systems.

Some of the more popular antivirus software programs for small businesses include these product lines:

- **Computer Associates eTrust** InoculateIT for Windows products -- www.ca.com

- **Network Associates McAfee** VirusScan and Net-Shield products -- www.mcafeeb2b.com/products/

- **Symantec Norton** AntiVirus products -- www.symantec.com/nav/

Resource Directory:
Want an easy way to recall the over 60 Web site references discussed in this book? Check out the Resource Directory, starting on page 261, for suggested Web sites that deal with PC hardware and peripherals, software applications and operating systems, data protection and other general small business technology information.

Tip #94

Go beyond file-level safeguards and invest in protection against other hostile threats.

✓ **Save on Soft Costs**

Save on Out-of-Pocket Expenses

Before small businesses became ultra-dependent on e-mail, Web browsing and other Internet applications, scanning for viruses at the file level was sufficient.

However, in the past few years, the Internet has been victimized by a whole new set of virus plagues that you need to protect against.

Composing Your Antivirus Software Shopping List

Fortunately, antivirus software vendors now integrate these protection features into their most recent product versions.

Beyond shielding your company from the dangers of viruses lurking in files, solutions should guard against common Internet-era virus threats.

- **Downloaded file protection** – blocks infected downloaded files from contaminating your system, even before reaching the target drive volume's file system

- **E-mail protection** – defends against problems coming in over the POP3 inbound mail protocol, viruses spreading outward from your company over the SMTP outbound mail protocol and viruses propagating internally throughout your company over the MAPI messaging interface

- **Heuristic pattern recognition** – detects viruses even *before* your antivirus software has a name for the virus; bases its alerts on knowledge of previous, similar virus activity

- **Hostile applet protection** – shields you from malicious programs reaching your system through ActiveX or Java applets (miniature software applications)

Antivirus Software for Servers

In addition to protection for your desktop PCs and notebooks, purchase and install antivirus software for any servers on your local area network (LAN).

In most cases, you'll need stand-alone products or add-on modules that cover your servers at a much more targeted level than mere file-level protection. Be sure to purchase and install specialized antivirus software for network applications, such as e-mail servers, proxy servers and Web servers.

Glossary:
Have you visited this book's Glossary yet? Get a quick refresher on over 160 terms used throughout this book – all those buzzwords and acronyms frequently thrown around by computer consultants and other techies. The Glossary, with extensive cross-references and chapter references, begins on page 231.

Tip #95

Update your antivirus software scanning engine and virus definitions.

✓ **Save on Soft Costs**

Save on Out-of-Pocket Expenses

Several years ago, a small business had no major need to update antivirus software all that regularly. If you updated antivirus software three or four times a year, your computer systems were fairly well-protected.

Instant Obsolescence

Courtesy of the dozens of new e-mail and Web-transported viruses discovered each month, those days of complacency are *long* gone. As recently as 1998, I still was recommending that small businesses update antivirus software once every four to six weeks. In this age of cyber-terrorism; however, you really cannot be well-protected against the newest viruses unless you update *every* desktop PC, notebook and server *at least* once a week. During a virus outbreak in your company, or during widely publicized national or international virus outbreaks, consider checking for antivirus software updates daily.

When I say updates, I'm talking about updating your antivirus software's signature, definition or pattern files. Most antivirus software vendors use a modular update/upgrade architecture, in which updates can be rolled out daily or weekly, while major version upgrades generally come out every 6 to 18 months. A more substantive part of the antivirus software, known as the scanning engine or core product code, will get minor version upgrades several times a year. But these are more like decimal releases, as opposed to major version upgrades, and generally are not sold as stand-alone upgrade products.

Unlike a conventional piece of shrink-wrapped software, antivirus software has a *very* short shelf life; it's generally obsolete before you even install it. After all, new viruses are discovered daily.

Purchase vs. Subscription

To combat this rapid software obsolescence, major antivirus software vendors have gravitated more and more toward subscription business models. This means you'll generally license the antivirus software for a certain length of time, during which you're entitled to unlimited product updates and, in many cases, unlimited product upgrades.

If the antivirus software on your systems is from shrink-wrapped retail products, or was bundled into the purchase price of the systems, you'll need to retrieve the license agreement that accompanied the software to see what it says about update and upgrade privileges. In many cases, you'll find that included update and upgrade privileges will span anywhere from 90 days to one year, *unless* you explicitly purchased an update subscription.

Again, first make sure your company is properly licensed for the antivirus software and updates. Then, just as important, see whether the software is properly installed and configured, *and* where updates are being applied regularly. These seemingly simple steps are the *essence* of avoiding many of the associated computer support costs with messy computer virus cleanups.

Internet-Era Protection

Finally, the severity of viruses coming in through your e-mail and Web browser programs now warrants additional protection at the application level -- which is designed to activate even before the virus threat reaches the antivirus software.

If you're in the small minority of businesses worldwide that doesn't depend on Microsoft Internet Explorer for Web browsing and Microsoft Outlook for e-mail, you'll need to check with the appropriate software vendor for the comparable software security patches and updates. However, if you're like the rest of us and depend on Microsoft Internet Explorer and Microsoft Outlook, read on for simple steps you can take to help fortify these programs against computer viruses.

The good news: It's gotten a *lot* easier for the non-techie to apply security updates to Microsoft Internet Explorer and Microsoft Outlook. However, the bad news is that now you may find it necessary to check for software updates to these programs almost weekly. Let these programs remain as is for longer periods, and you could be treading into dangerous, virus-bearing waters.

The Microsoft Office Product Updates and Microsoft Windows Update Web sites make it easy for you to tackle these security updates.

For step-by-step instructions on Microsoft Office Product Updates and Microsoft Windows Update, be sure to check out Tip #75 through Tip #77 in Chapter 5.

Tip #96

Learn how to check the status of your antivirus software and how to force a manual update.

✓ **Save on Soft Costs**

Save on Out-of-Pocket Expenses

This book is not designed to be a replacement for traditional computer books or software manuals. Rather, this book shows you opportunities for small business computer support cost savings, while warning you of common potential pitfalls that can cost your company *dearly* if ignored.

When Being Wrong is *Really* Dangerous

Over the years, I've met a great many small business owners who *thought* their antivirus software was up to date. But very few of them actually knew how to verify the date of the last update.

You usually can find this last updated information on various antivirus software programs by going to the Help pull-down menu and choosing the About command. If your antivirus software program is active or enabled, as well it should be, you probably also can right click on its icon in the Microsoft Windows Taskbar, at the bottom of your screen, and choose the About or Properties command.

But Our Sales Rep Said the Software Automatically Updates

Just as important, you cannot always depend on the software vendor's claim that the antivirus software will update itself automatically. Many antivirus software programs promise automated updates but frankly do not deliver.

This means you need to know how to force or download a manual update to the antivirus software program. Again, my goal here is not to overlap with your included software documentation, but rather to reinforce the critical necessity of keeping your antivirus software current. In most cases, you'll find easy-to-navigate file download links on the software vendor's Web site, so you can update your antivirus software.

Tip #97

Keep your antivirus software actively running at all times and know how to run a scan on demand.

✓ **Save on Soft Costs**

Save on Out-of-Pocket Expenses

Most antivirus software programs have both a reactive and proactive mode of operation.

When you use antivirus software reactively, the program *waits* for you to tell it to scan something for viruses, such as a diskette, a Microsoft Word document file or a local hard drive volume.

Checking for Viruses During Installation

During installation, most antivirus programs ask whether you want to run a complete scan of your system for viruses *before* proceeding.

After installation is complete, you usually can invoke this same complete system scan, either by launching the antivirus software program and initiating a scan manually, or by right clicking on something in Windows Explorer and choosing the scan for viruses or equivalent command. This procedure often is called scan on demand and, as the name implies, its fatal flaw is that it requires you to demand a virus scan before the antivirus software is called into action.

Automated Virus Scanning

Many antivirus software programs also have built-in scheduling mechanisms. This allows you, for example, to schedule a full system scan to occur after hours.

These antivirus methods do work, but they rely on your remembering to scan for viruses.

As we've seen throughout this book, automation is the cornerstone of *any* successful systems implementation. Nothing personal, but relying on manual intervention is a very dicey proposition, even under the best circumstances.

Antivirus Software in Its Proactive Mode

If you're working with dozens of Microsoft Word and Microsoft Excel files each day, you probably won't want to stop *every* time you open a file and run a virus scan manually *before* opening that file. Fortunately, there is a better way.

Antivirus software programs generally load in an active, enabled or resident mode when you boot up, and continue to run in the background, waiting for the opportunity to scan for viruses. This kind of operation is what allows you to be *pro*active about virus scanning.

Icon on the Windows Taskbar

An active antivirus software program normally will appear as an icon on your Windows Taskbar. And, just as you can with any icon on the Windows Taskbar, hovering on top of the antivirus software program icon will produce a little yellow popup ScreenTip telling you the name of the program.

It's *extremely* important for your antivirus program to appear on the Windows Taskbar as enabled, active or resident status. In fact, this mission-critical feature is what allows your antivirus software program automatically to intercept, red flag and block an infected file you are about to open from infiltrating your system. The only time antivirus software should be disabled is when you've explicitly been told to disable the antivirus software, such as when you are installing new software.

Free E-mail Newsletter:
Would you like a convenient way to keep up with new tips and techniques from Small Biz Tech Talk? Take control of your technology now! Subscribe to the free bi-weekly Tips newsletter at www.smallbiztechtalk.com

---

Tip #98

Limit your software downloads to those originating on major, highly reputable Web sites.

✓ **Save on Soft Costs**

Save on Out-of-Pocket Expenses

Ten years ago, one of the easiest ways to get a computer virus infection was to boot up inadvertently with an infected diskette.

Virus Infections in the Old Days

Although end users typically would deny, out of embarrassment, trying to install new software on their PCs, support professionals often saw clear evidence of what had transpired. More often than not, the user whose computer was infected had received a diskette, with a supposedly cool game, and was attempting to install the pirated software.

Internet-Era Virus Epidemics

Today, not many people pass around such files on diskettes. More commonly, the modern Internet-era version of this is downloading and installing a piece of unauthorized software – which also can create a license violation or break a key piece of software already on the PC.

Virus Prevention Training

As a result of this severe virus risk, users should be trained to avoid installing unauthorized, downloaded or noncommercial software on any PC, under *any* circumstances. Introducing new software programs into a stable PC/LAN environment is a task best left for the designated internal guru or professional computer consultant.

Even among authorized people in your office, these downloads should be confined to *extremely* reputable, major Web sites that have strong, vested business interests in preserving their reputations by distributing virus-free software downloads. Many companies even fold this prohibition into their company policy on acceptable Internet use.

For help getting started constructing such documents, see **How to Write Your Company's Internet Usage Policy** at
www.smallbiztechtalk.com/news/archives/tips070201-ht1.htm.

Tip #99

Be extremely suspicious of unsolicited e-mail messages with attachments.

✓ **Save on Soft Costs**

Save on Out-of-Pocket Expenses

E-mail attachments are a *fabulous* tool for whisking documents to a client across town or a supplier on the other side of the globe -- all at the speed of light.

And that's precisely the problem. The insidious creators of computer viruses have this same knowledge and exploit it. Albeit for nefarious, criminal purposes, virus creators know that e-mail attachments can be used to infect millions of computers around the world in a matter of mere minutes or hours.

Melissa

Before the Melissa virus in 1999, it was widely assumed that your friends, family members and business associates wouldn't e-mail you a computer virus -- or at least they wouldn't *knowingly* e-mail you an evil file payload.

However, with Melissa that all changed. Based on a simple Visual Basic routine, Melissa was the first widely circulated virus that spread itself by automatically e-mailing a copy of the virus to *everyone* in your Microsoft Outlook Address Book. Thus, it was precisely your closest contacts who got the virus and resulting infection.

It turned out that Melissa's weapon was that it was able to flood, or should I say *deluge*, Internet routers and mail servers with spurious messages that effectively shut down mail servers around the globe.

Unsolicited Attachments

The moral of the story: No matter who the sender of the e-mail message is, even if the attachments are from someone you know such as a coworker, spouse or boss, if you aren't expecting the file attachments, they could be *major* trouble.

If you think you need to look at the contents of the attachments, you always can reply back to the sender, or if possible contact the sender off line, and request him or her to resend the information in the body of the e-mail message.

For any messages that arouse your suspicions, don't forward the e-mail message. Delete the message immediately, then empty your Deleted Items folder in your e-mail program, as an added precaution.

Watch out for messages containing attachments from unknown sources, as well as messages originating from senders with odd return e-mail addresses. Be equally cautious of messages containing attachments that have SPAM-like subject lines, or message bodies with extremely poor grammar.

Just as important, you need to impart these precautions to *anyone* in your company who uses e-mail. Your users' vigilance can be an *extremely* effective weapon in preventing expensive virus contamination.

Remember, even if you are expecting the attachment, you should manually scan the file attachment before opening it, using the scan on demand methods discussed earlier in this chapter.

Companion CD-ROM

Are you ready to take your cost-savings to the next level, but you're at a loss for the *right* questions to ask? Check out the Companion CD-ROM for *What Your Computer Consultant Doesn't Want You to Know* -- with over 550 Action Items to get you started saving money right now.

The Action Items are presented in a variety of convenient file formats including Adobe Acrobat .pdf, HTML, Microsoft Word .doc and Microsoft Excel .xls. In addition, the Action Items are loaded up in a Microsoft Outlook Personal Folders File (.pst) -- ready for you to import into your Microsoft Outlook Tasks. The Companion CD-ROM also includes an electronic Resource Directory, recapping the book's suggested Web sites, that's all set for you to import into your Microsoft Internet Explorer Favorites list. Use the handy Action Item format to copy, paste and delegate -- while you tailor the money-saving program to your company's unique needs.

For more information on the Companion CD-ROM, see page 285.

Or visit www.smallbiztechtalk.com/tools/ to download sample Action Items or order the Companion CD-ROM.

Tip #100

Avoid forwarding virus hoax messages.

✓ **Save on Soft Costs**

Save on Out-of-Pocket Expenses

The cyber equivalent of chain letters, virus hoax messages often instill fear, attempt to separate the recipient from his or her wallet and clog up Internet routers, mail servers and e-mail inboxes.

Watch Out, Even If You Know the Sender

Don't let your guard down just because a friend, family member or colleague sent you the message. Avoid getting caught up in emotional excitement. The creators of hoax messages apparently have similar goals to those of virus creators: obstruct the flow of Internet data by overwhelming scarce resources. Most virus experts consider hoaxes just another strain of the common computer virus.

How Hoaxes Can Shut Down Your External Communications

One or two messages may be a mere annoyance. Several hundred or several thousand excess virus hoax messages flowing in or out of your company could effectively shut down your office's Internet access.

Keeping Up with Virus Outbreaks

Just like everything virus-related, you must keep current on the latest virus news. Here are some suggested Web sites:

- **Computer Associates Virus Information Center and Virus Encyclopedia** -- www3.ca.com/virus/

- **Network Associates Virus Information Library** -- vil.nai.com/vil/

- **Security Administrator** -- www.secadministrator.com

- **Symantec Security Response** -- www.symantec.com/avcenter/

- **TruSecure** -- www.trusecure.com

Tip #101

Invest in a deep, tape backup rotation system.

✓ **Save on Soft Costs**

Save on Out-of-Pocket Expenses

Scary Dormant Period for Viruses

Sometimes the effects of a virus are spotted, quarantined and cleaned up right away.

Other times, a virus may be festering for several days before even the most updated, sensitive, heuristic, virus scan tool detects the existence of a new virus.

Preparing to Roll Back

For this reason, you may need to roll back a set of files, folders or server volumes several days following a crippling virus attack. Most antivirus software programs do an excellent job of cleaning infections and make this exercise a rarity.

Yet, your best protection and peace of mind during a severe virus outbreak is knowing that you have the ability to roll back your data anywhere from one to several days to reach its pre-infection state.

For a full or selective rollback to work properly, you must be using a multi-tape data backup rotation scheme, much like the simple 20-tape system we discussed in Chapter 6.

Table of Tips:
Need a quick refresher on the 101 money-saving tips discussed in this book? Check out the Table of Tips, beginning on page 267, for a chapter-by-chapter recap and quick reference.

The Bottom Line

Left unchecked, computer viruses can cost your small business *enormous* amounts of money in lost data, unplanned downtime, hampered productivity, as well as interrupted communication and a damaged reputation with key business partners.

However, you can take many relatively simple steps to avoid becoming another virus infection statistic.

In this chapter, we looked at what features need to be in your antivirus solution, tips on how to maintain an effective antivirus system and best practices that need to filter down to your managers and PC users to establish a united front for combating Internet-era virus risks.

Resource Box

- **Computer Associates** -- www.ca.com

- **Computer Associates Virus Information Center and Virus Encyclopedia** -- www3.ca.com/virus/

- **Joshua Feinberg's Small Biz Tech Talk** -- www.smallbiztechtalk.com

- **Network Associates** -- www.nai.com

- **Network Associates McAfee VirusScan and NetShield products** -- www.mcafeeb2b.com/products/

- **Network Associates Virus Information Library** -- vil.nai.com/vil/

- **Security Administrator** -- www.secadministrator.com

- **Symantec Norton AntiVirus products** -- www.symantec.com/nav/

- **Symantec Security Response** -- www.symantec.com/avcenter/

- **TruSecure** -- www.trusecure.com

Glossary

A

ACPI (Advanced Configuration and Power Interface) – works in conjunction with the operating system and PC hardware; a part of the PC BIOS that coordinates various power management functions, such as automated power-off capabilities. See **Hardware** and **OS (Operating System)**. (Chapter 4)

Apple Mac OS – alternative to the Microsoft Windows family of operating systems; Apple Mac OS X v10 is Apple Computer's current software platform. See **Microsoft Windows**, **OS (Operating System)** and **Software**. (Chapter 4)

ASP (Application Service Provider) – based on the business model of outsourcing application installation, hosting, infrastructure, support and maintenance responsibilities; during 2000 and 2001, ASP industry was under extreme financial pressure, which ultimately led to the collapse of many prominent ASP industry leaders seeking to rent software as a service. See **Computer Support**, **Installation Expense**, **ISP (Internet Service Provider)**, **Maintenance Expense** and **Software**. (Chapter 5)

B

Battery Backup Unit – See **UPS (Uninterruptible Power Supply)**. (Chapter 7)

Blackout – utility power disturbance that can cause severe damage to your data files; utility input voltage dips to zero volts, resulting in a complete loss of electrical power; can be caused by overloaded circuits, utility pole or transformer damage, or utility companies conserving power during periods of exceptional, peak demand. (Chapter 7)

Broadband Internet Access – term commonly used to describe economically priced, high-speed Internet access delivered over cable modem, DSL (digital subscriber line) and satellite broadband technologies. See **Cable Modem**, **DSL (Digital Subscriber Line)** and **Internet Access**. (Chapter 5)

Brownout – utility power disturbance that can cause severe damage to your data files; results in a temporary reduction to a lower than normal level in utility line voltage supplied; a brownout of *very* short duration is also known as a sag; overloaded circuits sometimes cause brownouts; other times utility companies intentionally orchestrate rolling brownouts to conserve power during periods of exceptional, peak demand. See **Sag**. (Chapter 7)

Budget – forecast of what you plan to spend on a particular expense during an upcoming period of time; for example, a budget for technology purchases in the next 12 months. (All chapters)

Budget Surplus – when your actual expenses are *less* than the planned budgeted amount; as an example, if you budgeted $2,500 for telecommunications expenses during 2003 and your actual telecommunications expenses only totaled $1,900 at the end of 2003, you'd have a $600 budget surplus. (Chapter 1)

C

Cable Modem – a form of broadband telecommunications technology used for high-speed data transmission over existing coaxial television cabling; used primarily for delivering inexpensive, high-speed always-on Internet access; competes directly with DSL broadband Internet access offered largely by the regional telephone companies. See **Broadband Internet Access**, **DSL (Digital Subscriber Line)** and **Internet Access**. (Chapter 1 and Chapter 7)

Call Tag – service whereby a freight carrier, such as FedEx or UPS, picks up a package at your location, affixes a preaddressed return shipping label, and ships the package, at the requester's expense, back to the requester; analogous to reversing charges through a collect telephone call, call tags provide a convenient way for PC vendors to get a part returned to them at *their* expense; whenever requesting warranty replacement parts from a PC vendor, be sure to ask whether you're entitled to receive a call tag to cover the cost of returning the defective part. (Chapter 1)

Capital Expenditure – expense related to the purchase of a tangible asset, such as PC hardware; purchased to enhance the operations of your business, as opposed to tangible assets purchased for resale. (Chapter 1)

CAT3 (Category 3 Cable) – copper, unshielded twisted pair (UTP) cabling that can support voice and data communications at speeds up to 10Mbps for Ethernet networking. See **Ethernet Network Adapter**. (Chapter 2)

CAT5 (Category 5 Cable) – copper, unshielded twisted pair (UTP) cabling that can support voice and data communications at speeds up to 100Mbps and 1000Mbps for Ethernet networking. See **Ethernet Network Adapter**. (Chapter 2)

CD-RW Drive – an optical storage device that can be used to burn or write to blank CD-R media once and CD-RW (read-writable) media repeatedly, in addition to providing standard CD-ROM read-only functions; once completed, a CD-R disk generally can be read in standard CD-ROM drives, whereas a CD-RW disk usually can be read only from a similar or compatible CD-RW drive. (Chapter 2 and Chapter 6)

Chipset – a collection of integrated circuits functioning together as one unit; has become more compact as engineering advances allow more tasks to be executed on a single chip. (Chapter 1)

Clean Installation – a process of reformatting a PC hard drive from scratch by installing or reinstalling an operating system; after which you'll need to reinstall any applicable device drivers and third-party software applications, as well as restore data files and configuration settings; goal of a clean installation is to rebuild the PC configuration and arrive at a stable, more reliable state; generally preferable to, but typically more time-consuming than, an in-place installation. See **Device Driver**, **Hard Drive**, **In-Place Installation**, **OS (Operating System)** and **Software**. (Chapter 4)

Computer Consultant – a broad term used to describe an information technology (IT) professional whom small businesses retain for outsourced computer support services. See **Computer Support**, **IT (Information Technology)** and **Small Business**. (All chapters)

Computer Support – encompasses many routine information technology (IT) tasks and soft costs, such as needs analysis, product selection and procurement, installation, configuration, customization, training, documentation, as well as ongoing maintenance, troubleshooting and upgrading. See **Customization Expense**, **Installation Expense**, **IT (Information Technology)**, **Maintenance Expense**, **Procurement Expense**, **Soft Cost**, **Training for End Users**, **Training for the Internal Guru**, **Troubleshooting** and **Upgrade Expense**. (All chapters)

Cross-Ship – a PC hardware warranty replacement process where a PC hardware vendor ships out a replacement part *before* receiving the defective part back from the customer; depending on the estimated value of the part being cross-shipped, some PC hardware vendors require that a credit card number be provided as collateral for the replacement part advanced to the customer; a cross-shipped replacement part can dramatically reduce system downtime after a diagnosed hardware component failure. See **Hardware**. (Chapter 1)

CRT (Cathode Ray Tube) Monitor – a synonym for a conventional video monitor; the technical definition is actually the vacuum tube inside of the monitor; similar to that of a television set, a CRT produces an image when an electron beam strikes a phosphor-coated surface; the term CRT actually has come back into mainstream use in recent years to differentiate between the now more affordably priced, flat-screen LCD (Liquid Crystal Display) panel monitors and the older-style CRT-based monitors. See **LCD (Liquid Crystal Display) Flat Panel Monitor** and **Monitor**. (Chapter 1)

Customization Expense – computer support cost associated with tailoring a particular hardware, software or networking solution to a company's, department's or individual's unique business and technology needs. See **Computer Support**, **Hardware**, **Software** and **Network**. (Chapter 5)

Free E-mail Newsletter:
Would you like a convenient way to keep up with new tips and techniques from Small Biz Tech Talk? Take control of your technology now! Subscribe to the free bi-weekly Tips newsletter at www.smallbiztechtalk.com

---

D

DAT (Digital Audio Tape) Backup Drive – mass storage device that uses 4mm media based on digital audio tape; the current implementation of DAT-based tape backup drives is based on the DDS-4 standard, with a 20GB native/40GB compressed storage capacity; previous standards include DDS-3 for 12GB native/24GB compressed storage capacity and DDS-2 for 4GB native/8GB compressed storage capacity; offers high-speed backup with relatively low-cost media, but at a higher hardware purchase cost than Travan tape backup drives. See **Hardware, Tape Backup Drive** and **Travan Tape Backup Drive**. (Chapter 6)

Database Software (Relational) – software application that stores structured information in fields, records and related tables; besides Microsoft's database software, many small businesses use software applications based on relational database engines from IBM, Oracle and Sybase. See **Microsoft Access**, **Microsoft SQL Server**, **Small Business** and **Software**. (Chapter 3, Chapter 4 and Chapter 6)

Data Line Power Protection – a device that sits between various telecommunications cables and your PC hardware to protect your PC hardware from utility line voltage spikes and surges; although products need first to be grounded properly, data line power protection devices can interface with many connectors including RJ-11 and RJ-14 for telephone circuits, RJ-45 for network cabling and RS-232 for serial lines. See **Hardware**, **Network**, **Serial Port**, **Spike** and **Surge**. (Chapter 2 and Chapter 7)

Data Restoration – regenerating and copying data stored on archive or backup media back to their original or an alternative target folder path. See **Tape Backup Drive**. (Chapter 1, Chapter 5, Chapter 6 and Chapter 8)

Dedicated Circuit – also commonly known as a home run, a broad term used by cable installers and electricians to describe a telephone or networking cable, or electrical circuit, isolated for exclusive use and containing no in-line splices between the place utility service enters the office and the jack or outlet terminations. See **Home Run** and **Network**. (Chapter 2 and Chapter 7)

Depreciation Expense – a cost incurred as you allocate the loss in value of certain technology assets during the assets' useful life; for advice on estimating and calculating depreciation expenses, consult an accounting professional. (Chapter 1 and Chapter 2)

Desktop PC – personal computer that usually remains stationary and is largely characterized by its physical presence on or near a desk, as well as its use by one person at a time; two other models of PCs include the notebook computer, characterized by its mobility, small size and light weight, and the server, predominantly used to share resources among multiple users. See **Notebook PC** and **Server**. (All chapters)

Device Driver – a small piece of critical software code that allows a hardware device or component to communicate with a specific operating system. See **Hardware, OS (Operating System)** and **Software**. (Chapter 1, Chapter 2, Chapter 5 and Chapter 6)

Device Driver Signing – a quality-assurance program Microsoft initiated with Microsoft Windows 2000 to require device drivers to contain a digital signature to prove authenticity of their author and ensure that it's been tested by Microsoft Hardware Quality Labs; protects users from inadvertently installing device drivers that can cause system instability. See **Device Driver** and **Microsoft Windows**. (Chapter 4)

DLT (Digital Linear Tape) Backup Drive – mass storage device that uses 0.5-inch-wide media; DLT-based tape backup drives offer superior throughput and capacity compared to DAT-based tape backup drives; however, these advantages come at price that's generally out of the range of most small business technology budgets; current Super DLT (SDLT) implementation offers 110GB of native and 220GB of compressed storage capacity. See **DAT (Digital Audio Tape) Backup Drive, Small Business** and **Tape Backup Drive**. (Chapter 6)

Dongle Cable – an adapter used to attach a telephone or network cable to a notebook system PCMCIA adapter, mainly used with older PCMCIA notebook modems and network adapters; highly prone to loss and breakage; has been supplanted largely by replacements such as the 3Com XJACK and Xircom RealPort connectors; also sometimes referred to as a pigtail cable. See **Modem, NIC (Network Interface Card), Notebook PC** and **PCMCIA Slot**. (Chapter 2)

Downloaded File Protection – antivirus protection that blocks infected files downloaded from the Internet from contaminating your systems, even before reaching the target drive volume's file system. See **Virus**. (Chapter 8)

DSL (Digital Subscriber Line) – broadband telecommunications technology used for delivering high-speed data transmission over existing copper twisted-pair wire installed between your telephone company's central office and your office; used primarily for delivering inexpensive, high-speed, always-on Internet access; competes directly with shared broadband cable modem Internet access offered largely by cable television companies. See **Broadband Internet Access**, **Cable Modem** and **Internet Access**. (Chapter 1, Chapter 2, Chapter 5 and Chapter 7)

E

E-mail – abbreviation for electronic mail; software that allows you to send and receive messages over a network from one user to another user or group of users. See **Network** and **Software**. (All chapters)

E-mail Protection – antivirus protection that blocks infected file attachments you receive over e-mail from contaminating your systems, even before reaching the target drive volume's file system. See **E-mail** and **Virus**. (Chapter 8)

Employee Productivity – broad term describing an individual staff member's ability to create something of tangible value; if technology is implemented effectively, related systems always should facilitate and positively influence employee productivity. (Chapter 1, Chapter 3, Chapter 4, Chapter 7 and Chapter 8)

Entrepreneur – a risk taker; term usually used interchangeably with small business owner. See **Small Business**. (All chapters)

Equipment Protection Guarantee – a standard customer service policy of manufacturers of power protection products; backs up claims of product protection from power disturbances with a financial guarantee; known by several names assigned for marketing and branding purposes, such as Equipment Protection Policy (APC) and Ultimate Lifetime Insurance (Tripp Lite). (Chapter 7)

Ethernet Network Adapter – due to the market dominance of Ethernet networks, an Ethernet network adapter has become largely synonymous with the more general term network adapter or network interface card. See **Network** and **NIC (Network Interface Card)**. (Chapter 1, Chapter 2, Chapter 4 and Chapter 7)

Expansion Slot – an opening in a computer motherboard that allows you to insert an expansion card and extend the capabilities of the system; the current mainstream generation of expansion slots and expansion cards is based on 32-bit PCI interfaces; the much older, legacy generation of expansion slots and expansion cards is based on 16-bit ISA interfaces. See **Motherboard**. (Chapter 1 and Chapter 2)

F

Firmware – a hybrid between software and hardware in which certain instruction sets for a particular hardware device are programmed or burned into nonvolatile read-only memory (ROM); firmware often can be updated through a process known as flashing the firmware chip, protecting your hardware investment with an upgradeable architecture. See **Hardware** and **Software**. (Chapter 1, Chapter 2 and Chapter 4)

G

Graphics Accelerator – often used synonymously with the terms "video display adapter" or "video graphics adapter," it usually has its own embedded processor and dedicated RAM to increase graphics performance; in newer PCs, the chipset of the graphics accelerator often built into the system's motherboard. See **Chipset**, **Motherboard**, **RAM (Random Access Memory)** and **Video Display Adapter**. (Chapter 1 and Chapter 4)

H

Hard Drive – mechanism that drives the mass storage device responsible for reading and writing most of the data involved in the operation of desktop PCs, notebooks and servers; also commonly referred to as hard disk or hard disk drive; generally the fastest and largest-capacity storage device in most systems. See **Desktop PC**, **Notebook PC** and **Server**. (All chapters)

Hardware – the physical, tangible equipment and components used to power computing devices, as opposed to the software that is stored and runs on the hardware equipment and components; common hardware includes desktop PCs, notebooks, servers, printers, modems, network cards and routers. See **Desktop PC**, **Modem**, **NIC (Network Interface Card)**, **Notebook PC**, **Server** and **Software**. (All chapters)

Hardware Compatibility List (HCL) – a free online resource at www.microsoft.com/hcl that lists hardware manufacturers, product models and Microsoft-confirmed compatibility and certification testing across different versions of Microsoft Windows operating systems; most third-party vendors maintain similar resources on their Web sites. See **Hardware**, **Microsoft Windows** and **OS (Operating System)**. (Chapter 2)

Heuristic Pattern Recognition – antivirus protection that detects viruses even before your antivirus software has a name for the virus; bases its alerts on knowledge of previous, similar virus activity. See **Software** and **Virus**. (Chapter 8)

Home Run – See **Dedicated Circuit**. (Chapter 2 and Chapter 7)

Hostile Applet Protection – antivirus protection that blocks malicious Web-based applets written in Java and ActiveX from damaging your systems, even before data reach the target drive volume's file system. See **Virus**. (Chapter 8)

HTML (Hypertext Markup Language) – the authoring and formatting language used to build pages for the World Wide Web (WWW). See **Web Browser Software**. (Chapter 3)

I

In-Place Installation – reinstalling an operating system on top of an existing operating system installation; while generally a faster procedure, an in-place installation is not nearly as thorough as a clean installation. See **Clean Installation** and **OS (Operating System)**. (Chapter 4)

Inside Wiring – the telephone cabling inside your office, between the telephone service's entry point at the NID (Network Interface Device) and each telephone modem jack's termination. See **Modem** and **NID (Network Interface Device)**. (Chapter 2)

Installation Expense – computer support cost associated with removing a product from packaging, verifying that product contents match the purchase order, moving the product to the desired physical location and setting up the product for its intended purpose. See **Computer Support**. (All chapters)

Integrator – professional services firm or organization, sometimes part of a large company, that specializes in making heterogeneous computer systems work together; also commonly referred to as a network integrator or systems integrator; many computer consultants who aren't self-employed work for an integrator. See **Computer Consultant** and **Network Integrator**. (Chapter 1)

Internal Guru – a term believed to be coined and later popularized extensively by small business technology expert Joshua Feinberg; someone who works for, manages or owns a small business who has become the de facto computer person in addition to his or her alleged real job; internal gurus can come from a wide variety of occupations, including accounting, administration, finance, operations and sales; generally the main tactical liaison between a small business and an external consultant; position combines the attributes of a PC power user with responsibilities of managerial or quasi-managerial role. See **Computer Consultant**, **Power User** and **Small Business**. (All chapters)

Internet Access – the online equivalent of the telephone dial tone; a broad term describing a connection to the global Internet for Web browsing, sending and receiving e-mail messages, and other related Internet-enabled applications; common Internet access forms include dial-up, broadband DSL, broadband cable and ISDN; businesses with larger technology budgets opt for more reliable, higher-performance Internet access via Frame Relay and T1/T3 services. See **Broadband Internet Access**, **Cable Modem**, **DSL (Digital Subscriber Line)**, **E-mail**, **ISP (Internet Service Provider)** and **Web Browser Software**. (Chapter 1, Chapter 5, Chapter 6 and Chapter 8)

Investment – the general framework in which most small business technology expenses should be evaluated; as you would any investment, consider how you would quantify and measure benefits so you can forecast and monitor return on investment (ROI); most technology investments in this book are intended to increase productivity while reducing out-of-pocket technology expenses, soft computer support costs and unplanned system downtime and related business interruption. See **Computer Support**, **Employee Productivity**, **ROI (Return on Investment)** and **Small Business**. (Chapter 1, Chapter 2 and Chapter 5)

ISP (Internet Service Provider) – a telecommunications service company that sells Internet access and related value-added services such as Web, e-mail, e-commerce and applications hosting. See **E-mail** and **Internet Access**. (Chapter 2, Chapter 5 and Chapter 6)

ISV (Independent Software Vendor) – develops and usually also markets such software products as applications, operating systems or utilities. See **OS (Operating System)** and **Software**. (Chapter 5)

IT (Information Technology) – a broad term used to encompass a branch of technology involving the application of hardware, software, services, networks and processes to manage information assets, generally for solving business problems; also often referred to as information services (IS), or in the past as management information sciences (MIS) or electronic data processing (EDP). See **Hardware**, **Network** and **Software**. (All chapters)

K

Kernel – the innermost, critical and vulnerable core internal services of an operating system (OS); in contrast to the outermost visible portion of software, usually referred to as the user interface (UI) or shell. See **OS (Operating System)** and **Software**. (Chapter 4)

L

LAN (Local Area Network) – set of computer systems and peripheral devices connected for sharing resources and providing near-instantaneous communications; today's small business LANs are typically physically connected using Ethernet network adapters and Category 5 cabling; when extended to one or more additional geographic locations, can become a metropolitan area network (MAN) or wide area network (WAN). See **CAT5 (Category 5 Cable)**, **Ethernet Network Adapter**, **Network**, **Peripheral Device**, **Small Business** and **WAN (Wide Area Network)**. (All chapters)

LCD (Liquid Crystal Display) Flat Panel Monitor – display technology created by two polarized sheets with liquid crystal solution in between; used in notebook computers for many years before price allowed for rapid proliferation into the desktop PC display market; differentiating features include low power consumption, light weight and thin footprint; contrasts with more conventional, older-style CRT-based monitors. See **CRT (Cathode Ray Tube) Monitor**, **Desktop PC** and **Notebook PC**. (Chapter 1)

License Agreement – a legal contract to run a given software program under a specific set of restrictions; similar to a rental agreement; often referred to as an end user license agreement or EULA. See **Site License** and **Software**. (Chapter 5 and Chapter 8)

Line Conditioner – power protection product that helps to ensure that utility power flowing into the protected hardware falls within pre-configured ranges; used to clean up interference coming from noisy utility service; also commonly referred to as a power conditioner or automatic voltage regulator. See **Hardware**. (Chapter 7)

Linux – an open source, freely distributed and supported, extendable operating system variant of UNIX created by Linus Torvaldis; developed and continues to be expanded upon by many individuals, companies and organizations worldwide. See **OS (Operating System)** and **UNIX**. (Chapter 4)

M

Mail Merge – an office automation productivity software feature common in word processing programs such as Microsoft Word; provides the ability to create customized documents such as envelopes, form letters and mailing labels using database records from several sources; has evolved into an interoperability tool allowing for use of data from multiple software applications of various independent software vendors (ISVs). See **Database Software (Relational)**, **ISV (Independent Software Vendor)**, **Microsoft Word**, **Software** and **Word Processing Software**. (Chapter 3 and Chapter 5)

Maintenance Expense – computer support cost associated with keeping software and hardware functioning optimally, reliably and securely; in a Microsoft-centric small business computing environment, software maintenance predominantly will involve keeping systems current with various service releases (SRs), service packs (SPs) and virus definition updates. See **Computer Support**, **Hardware**, **Small Business**, **Software**, **SP/SR (Service Pack/Service Release)** and **Virus**. (Chapter 1, Chapter 3, Chapter 5, Chapter 6 and Chapter 8)

Microsoft Access – a relational database software application for small workgroups; database format that can be scaled up to or work in conjunction with other, more robust, server-based, relational database software applications such as Microsoft SQL Server; part of the Microsoft Office family. See **Database Software (Relational)**, **Microsoft Office**, **Microsoft SQL Server**, **Server** and **Software**. (Chapter 3 and Chapter 4)

Microsoft Excel – a software application based on spreadsheets, organized by cells, rows, columns, worksheets and workbooks; part of the Microsoft Office family and included with all versions of Microsoft Office. See **Microsoft Office**, **Software** and **Spreadsheet Software**. (Chapter 1, Chapter 3, Chapter 4, Chapter 6 and Chapter 8)

Microsoft Exchange Server – a server-side back office software application that provides the e-mail messaging and collaborative backbone engine for using Microsoft Outlook companywide. See **E-mail, Microsoft Outlook, Server** and **Software**. (Chapter 6)

Microsoft Internet Explorer – Web browser software, often the target of malicious hacker attempts to exploit vulnerabilities; to be kept secure, needs frequent updating through Windows Update; commonly abbreviated as IE. See **Web Browser Software** and **Windows Update**. (Chapter 4, Chapter 5, Chapter 6 and Chapter 8)

Microsoft Office – an integrated suite of bundled software applications; under Microsoft Office 2000, the offerings included Standard, Small Business, Professional and Premium Editions; under Microsoft Office XP, the offerings include Standard, Small Business (bundled only with new PCs), Professional, Developer and Professional Special Edition; encompasses Microsoft Word, Microsoft Excel, Microsoft Outlook, Microsoft Publisher, Microsoft Access, Microsoft PowerPoint, Microsoft FrontPage, SharePoint Team Services, IntelliMouse Explorer and Developer Tools. See **Microsoft Access, Microsoft Excel, Microsoft Outlook, Microsoft PowerPoint, Microsoft Publisher, Microsoft Word, Small Business** and **Software**. (All chapters)

Microsoft Office Product Updates – a free Web-based tool, similar to Windows Update, that helps you stay up to date with the latest Microsoft Office patches, enhancements and service releases; automatically inventories your Microsoft Office installation, makes recommendations for updates, packages these updates together into a single download and assists with the download and installation of updates. See **Microsoft Office, SP/SR (Service Pack/Service Release), Web Browser Software** and **Windows Update**. (Chapter 3 and Chapter 8)

Microsoft Open License – a flexible software discount site-licensing program for small and mid-sized businesses with a minimum of five PCs. See **License Agreement, Site License, Small Business** and **Software**. (Chapter 5)

Microsoft Outlook – a client/workstation software application that provides the front-end e-mail messaging, group scheduling, contact management and collaboration functions when using Microsoft Exchange Server on the backbone for companywide messaging and collaboration; can be used on both networked and non-networked PCs, without Microsoft Exchange Server, for basic Internet e-mail and stand-alone personal information management; part of the Microsoft Office family; also included with Microsoft Exchange Server; included with all editions of Microsoft Office. See **E-mail, Microsoft Exchange Server, Microsoft Office, Network** and **Software**. (Chapter 1, Chapter 3, Chapter 4, Chapter 6 and Chapter 8)

Microsoft Outlook Personal Folders File – the basic file format (.pst) for data storage when using Microsoft Outlook without Microsoft Exchange Server or when used in addition to a Microsoft Exchange Server connection but with individual data stored separately; a crucial file that needs to be backed up regularly; used for archiving and transferring data during PC system upgrades and system replacements; can be stored on a local hard drive or network-based shared server folder. See **Hard Drive, Microsoft Exchange Server, Microsoft Outlook, Network** and **Server**. (Chapter 3 and Chapter 6)

Microsoft PowerPoint – a presentation graphics software application used primarily for creating and presenting slideshows during seminars, speeches and training classes; part of the Microsoft Office suite. See **Microsoft Office** and **Software**. (Chapter 3)

Microsoft Publisher – a desktop publishing software application used primarily by small businesses for creating documents such as newsletters, brochures, advertising collateral and stationery; part of the Microsoft Office suite. See **Microsoft Office, Small Business** and **Software**. (Chapter 3)

Microsoft SBS (Small Business Server) – a networking solution for small businesses with 5 to 50 PCs in a single location; an integrated suite of client/server software applications that includes file and printer sharing (Microsoft Windows 2000 Server), messaging and collaboration (Microsoft Outlook and Microsoft Exchange Server), database management (Microsoft SQL Server), shared Internet access, caching and security (Microsoft Internet Security and Acceleration Server), Web hosting (Microsoft Internet Information Services) and network faxing. See **Database Software (Relational), Internet Access, Microsoft Exchange Server, Microsoft Outlook, Microsoft SQL Server, Microsoft Windows, Network, Server, Small Business** and **Software**. (Chapter 6)

Microsoft SQL Server – a robust, client/server relational database software application that can scale up from small workgroups to major, enterprise, mission-critical needs; after outgrowing a workgroup relational database software application such as Microsoft Access, a small business often will migrate the database to Microsoft SQL Server. See **Database Software (Relational), Microsoft Access, Server, Small Business** and **Software**. (Chapter 6)

Microsoft Windows – family of operating systems (OS's), launched by Microsoft in the mid-1980s, which only began to gain mass market acceptance several years later with 16-bit versions based on Microsoft Windows 3.x; several 32-bit versions of Microsoft Windows are used by small businesses including various versions of Microsoft Windows 95, Microsoft Windows NT 4, Microsoft Windows 98, Microsoft Windows 2000, Microsoft Windows Millennium Edition (Me) and Microsoft Windows XP. See **OS (Operating System)** and **Small Business**. (All chapters)

Microsoft Windows CE – a specialty version of the Microsoft Windows operating system originally designed for handheld computers based on Microsoft's Pocket PC design specification; largest major competitor is the Palm OS. See **Microsoft Windows, OS (Operating System)** and **Palm OS**. (Chapter 2)

Microsoft Windows Desktop – a part of Microsoft Windows operating systems that users see when all Windows are either closed or minimized; most often used to create, organize and display a series of Shortcuts pointing to commonly used software, file folders and other local and network resources. See **Microsoft Windows, Network, OS (Operating System), Shortcut** and **Software**. (Chapter 4)

Microsoft Word – a word processing software application; part of the Microsoft Office suite; included with all versions of Microsoft Office. See **Microsoft Office, Software** and **Word Processing Software**. (All chapters)

Modem – peripheral device used for point-to-point communication between two computer systems; term originally coined to describe a modulator/demodulator device that performs two-way conversion between digital and analog signals required for data transmission over the public switched telephone network (PSTN); definition extended to include non-analog devices functioning in a bridged capacity such as a cable modem, DSL modem and ISDN modem. See **Cable Modem, DSL (Digital Subscriber Line)** and **Peripheral Device**. (Chapter 1, Chapter 2, Chapter 4 and Chapter 7)

Monitor – synonymous with video monitor, two main kinds used by small businesses based on CRT (cathode ray tube) and LCD (liquid crystal display). See **CRT (Cathode Ray Tube) Monitor** and **LCD (Liquid Crystal Display) Flat Panel Monitor**. (Chapter 1)

Motherboard – the main printed circuit board inside a computer system that integrates the processor, RAM, system bus expansion slots, and various chipsets, controllers, input/output ports and interfaces. See **Chipset**, **Expansion Slot** and **RAM (Random Access Memory)**. (Chapter 1)

N

Network – a system of interconnected computer systems and related devices that communicate with one another; common networks used by small businesses include the local area network (LAN), wide area network (WAN) and Internet. See **LAN (Local Area Network)**, **Small Business** and **WAN (Wide Area Network)**. (All chapters)

Network Integrator – a computer services business that designs, installs and maintains heterogeneous computer systems and software. See **Integrator** and **Software**. (Chapter 1)

NIC (Network Interface Card) – a printed circuit board, adapter card or the underlying supporting chipset that snaps into the motherboard of a desktop PC, notebook, or server and transmits and receives packets on a network; used to connect to networks including a local area network (LAN), wide area network (WAN), or a broadband network for high-speed cable modem or DSL-based Internet access; most common NIC used by small businesses is the 10/100Mbps Ethernet adapter. See **Broadband Internet Access**, **Cable Modem**, **Chipset**, **Desktop PC**, **DSL (Digital Subscriber Line)**, **Ethernet Network Adapter**, **LAN (Local Area Network)**, **Motherboard**, **Notebook PC**, **Server** and **WAN (Wide Area Network)**. (Chapter 1, Chapter 2, Chapter 4 and Chapter 7)

NID (Network Interface Device) – telephone company point of demarcation ("demarc") where circuits and service are terminated, and where your responsibility for inside wiring begins. See **Inside Wiring**. (Chapter 2)

NOS (Network Operating System) – an OS (operating system) designed for communications between networked computer systems; popular NOS's include Apple Mac OS, Linux, Microsoft Windows NT/2000 and Novell NetWare. See **Apple Mac OS**, **Linux**, **Microsoft Windows**, **Network** and **OS (Operating System)**. (Chapter 6)

Notebook PC – also commonly referred to as a laptop; a personal computer characterized by battery power, mobility, small size, light weight and LCD monitor; other kinds of computers include the desktop PC and server. See **Desktop PC, LCD (Liquid Crystal Display) Flat Panel Monitor** and **Server**. (All chapters)

O

Offline Files – a feature and accompanying wizard in Microsoft Windows 2000 Professional and Microsoft Windows XP Professional that allows you to continue to access network-based files and folders *after* you've physically disconnected from the network server. See **Microsoft Windows**, **Network** and **Server**. (Chapter 4)

On-Site Warranty – hardware product warranty in which a hardware manufacturer's tech support department will diagnose a problem over the telephone with the user and, at the discretion of the hardware manufacturer, dispatch a technician with parts to make necessary repairs under terms of the product warranty; in contrast to a return-to-depot warranty, in which the hardware must be shipped, generally at the buyer's expense, or delivered in person, to a factory-authorized repair center for warranty service. See **Hardware**. (Chapter 1 and Chapter 5)

OS (Operating System) – crucial software program that provides the platform upon which other software applications run, as well as the underlying infrastructure between hardware devices, software applications and the user interface; popular OS's used by small businesses include Apple Mac OS, Linux and several versions of Microsoft Windows. See **Apple Mac OS, Hardware, Linux, Microsoft Windows, Software** and **UNIX**. (All chapters)

P

Palm OS – a specialty operating system designed for handheld computers manufactured and marketed by Palm and others; largest major competitor is Microsoft Windows CE. See **Microsoft Windows CE, OS (Operating System)** and **PDA (Personal Digital Assistant)**. (Chapter 2)

Parallel Port – hardware interface, usually built into a computer system's motherboard, that allows for one- or two-way communication with a peripheral device; most often utilized by printers; eventually may be rendered obsolete by the USB port. See **Hardware, Motherboard, Peripheral Device** and **USB (Universal Serial Bus) Port**. (Chapter 1 and Chapter 2)

PCMCIA Slot – similar in function to a desktop PC or server expansion slot; most often found in notebook and handheld computers; used for credit-card-sized hardware devices such as modems and network cards; PCMCIA acronym comes from the Personal Computer Memory Card International Association that established the first standard in 1993; later came to be known as a PC Card slot; newer 32-bit CardBus standard provides for greater performance and lower power consumption. See **Expansion Slot, Hardware, Modem, NIC (Network Interface Card)** and **Notebook PC**. (Chapter 2)

PDA (Personal Digital Assistant) – a handheld, pocket-sized computer generally designed for the Microsoft Windows CE or Palm OS platforms. See **Microsoft Windows CE** and **Palm OS**. (Chapter 2)

Peripheral Device – a hardware device that's separate from the system unit; common external peripherals used by small businesses include digital cameras, modems, printers and scanners. See **Hardware** and **Modem**. (Chapter 1, Chapter 2, Chapter 4, Chapter 5 and Chapter 7)

Physical Security – all required measures taken to maintain control over access to facilities housing IT assets and prevent unauthorized individuals from inadvertently or deliberately accessing, tampering with or misappropriating PC systems, telecommunications equipment, backup media and data cabling; protecting facilities and IT assets from physical risks such as theft, fire, water, wind damage and earthquakes. See **IT (Information Technology)**. (Chapter 6)

Plug and Play – the ability and underlying design philosophy for an operating system to identify automatically that new hardware has been added to a PC, to pinpoint what that hardware device is, and to install and configure automatically the necessary device driver, system files and system resources to make the new hardware device function with the operating system and supporting, related, PC hardware components; for Plug and Play to function properly, the PC BIOS, operating system and hardware device all must support Plug and Play. See **Device Driver, Hardware** and **OS (Operating Systems)**. (Chapter 2)

Power User – an employee in your company who's a more skilled PC user than most others but hasn't been entrusted with the responsibility of being the designated Internal Guru. See **Internal Guru**. (Chapter 1, Chapter 4 and Chapter 6)

Processor Clock Speed – traditionally measured in Megahertz (abbreviated Mhz) processor technology has progressed exponentially, with many processors exceeding speeds of 1,000Mhz and advertised as Gigahertz speed (abbreviated Ghz); a measure of central processing unit (CPU) power and performance, but not necessarily a measure of overall system performance, due to other possible component bottlenecks. (Chapter 1)

Procurement Expense – a computer support expense related to the research into purchasing IT assets, vendor selection, purchase order (PO) execution, order tracking and inspection of shipped goods for conformance to order specifications. See **Computer Support** and **IT (Information Technology)**. (Chapter 2)

Pull-Down Menu – part of a software application's user interface (UI) typically toward the top of the display; lists available commands, which give instructions to the software program; although pull-down menus are generally more comprehensive in nature, Toolbars and Toolbar buttons often provide a simpler way of accessing the more commonly used commands and as such are a better choice for training end users. See **Software**, **Toolbar** and **Training for End Users**. (Chapter 3, Chapter 4 and Chapter 5)

R

RAM (Random Access Memory) – a crucial hardware component upgrade that can increase dramatically the performance of your PC for a very nominal investment; very high-speed, temporary or volatile memory with contents that vanish when your system is powered off or crashes; faster than hard drive storage by a magnitude of thousands as RAM speed is measured in nanoseconds (ns) while hard drive speed is measured in milliseconds (ms); the more RAM your computer has, the less likely the hard drive will have to step in and supplement RAM with the hard drive's much slower paging file. See **Hard Drive**, **Hardware** and **Investment**. (Chapter 1, Chapter 2 and Chapter 4)

Reboot – the process of shutting down and restarting a computer; purges out the contents of RAM and often rids a computer of transient software errors, providing a clean-up of sorts; a cold reboot, in which you shut down the computer and power it off, before powering back up again, is even more cleansing than a warm reboot, in which you shut down and restart without removing the computer's power source. See **RAM (Random Access Memory)** and **Software**. (Chapter 2, Chapter 3, Chapter 4 and Chapter 8)

Recovery Console – a troubleshooting tool in Microsoft Windows 2000 Professional that can be used when your system won't boot up on its own; can save several hours of anguish when trying to recover a damaged OS configuration; dramatically reduces the time required to fix many OS problems; allows you to check and repair a hard drive's boot sector and master boot record and repair problems related to OS services and device drivers; gives you a much better chance of fixing a damaged configuration, without having to resort to a productivity hampering and expensive OS rebuild; sometimes abbreviated as RC. See **Device Driver**, **Hard Drive**, **Microsoft Windows** and **OS (Operating System)**. (Chapter 4)

Registry – a hierarchical database used to store configuration information for user preferences, installed hardware, OS configuration choices and software application settings; every version of Microsoft Windows since Microsoft Windows 95 relies on a Registry. See **Hardware**, **Microsoft Windows**, **OS (Operating System)** and **Software**. (Chapter 3, Chapter 4 and Chapter 5)

Relational Database – see **Database Software (Relational)**. (Chapter 3, Chapter 4 and Chapter 5)

Remote Access – a way to extend the core services of a network to users at remote sites; often achieved by using analog telephone lines and standard dial-up modems, while relying on either built-in remote access features in the Microsoft Windows OS or purchasing a third-party remote control software application, which uses a different technology than remote access. See **Microsoft Windows**, **Modem**, **Network**, **OS (Operating System)** and **Software**. (Chapter 2 and Chapter 5)

ROI (Return on Investment) – a key metric for forecasting and measuring the concrete benefits of a specific technology investment. See **Investment**. (Chapter 1)

S

Safe Boot Mode – supported in most recent 32-bit versions of Microsoft Windows, except Microsoft Windows NT 4; a troubleshooting tool that can be used when your system won't boot up; bypasses startup configuration and loads a very limited set of OS files, device drivers and core OS services. See **Device Driver**, **Microsoft Windows** and **OS (Operating System)**. (Chapter 4)

Sag – utility power disturbance that can cause severe damage to your hardware and data files; utility power drops and results in a brownout of very short duration. See **Brownout** and **Hardware**. (Chapter 7)

Scanning Engine – the less frequently updated part of antivirus software's two-part modular structure; also known as core product code, a scanning engine gets minor version upgrades several times a year; updated less frequently than signature, pattern or virus definition files. See **Signature File**, **Software** and **Virus**. (Chapter 8)

Scheduled Task Wizard – the front-end graphical user interface (GUI) for the Task Scheduler service; allows you to write simple batch files that can be scheduled to run at certain dates and times; can use the Scheduled Task Wizard to set up a simple, automated, data replication system with basically no programming; requires Microsoft Internet Explorer 5.x or higher. See **Microsoft Internet Explorer**. (Chapter 6)

ScreenTips – feature in Microsoft Office that allows users to quickly recall the function of each Toolbar button; to access a ScreenTip, leave the mouse pointer hovering on a Toolbar button for a few seconds without clicking the mouse button. See **Microsoft Office** and **Toolbar**. (Chapter 3)

Serial Port – hardware interface, usually built into a computer system's motherboard, that allows for two-way communication with a peripheral device; most often used by digital cameras, external modems, label printers and UPS interfaces; can come in 9-pin or 25-pin configurations, although the 9-pin configuration has become much more popular; eventually may be made obsolete by the USB port. See **Hardware, Modem, Motherboard, Peripheral Device, UPS (Uninterruptible Power Supply)** and **USB (Universal Serial Bus) Port**. (Chapter 2 and Chapter 7)

Server – any computing device or peripheral on a network designed to provide shared services and resources to network users; primarily characterized by multi-user usage, as compared to a desktop or notebook PC; common servers include the file, printer, e-mail messaging and collaboration, Web, proxy and database server. See **Database Software (Relational)**, **Desktop PC**, **E-mail**, **Network**, **Notebook PC** and **Peripheral Device**. (All chapters)

Shortcut – a graphical user interface (GUI) icon on the Microsoft Windows Desktop or Start Menu used for launching a software application or other OS object; can reduce user confusion and accompanying computer support costs by placing Shortcuts on the Microsoft Windows Desktop for the most commonly used software applications – and removing any superfluous Shortcuts for software applications not used. See **Computer Support**, **Microsoft Windows Desktop**, **OS (Operating System)** and **Software**. (Chapter 4 and Chapter 5)

Signature File – the more frequently updated part of antivirus software's two-part modular structure; also known as a pattern or virus definition file; usually updated several times a month and immediately after a new major virus outbreak. See **Scanning Engine**, **Software** and **Virus**. (Chapter 8)

Site License – a program in which you contract for a specific quantity of software licenses for a certain duration of time, many times with free update and upgrade privileges, and receive a discount in return. See **License Agreement**, **Microsoft Open License**, **Software** and **Upgrade Expense**. (Chapter 5 and Chapter 8)

SLA (Service Level Agreement) – a customer service pledge and guarantee by a technology provider, telecommunications firm, ASP or ISP to uphold certain performance standards that can be precisely monitored and logged; not meeting an SLA typically carries a financial penalty. See **ASP (Application Service Provider)**, **ISP (Internet Service Provider)** and **Technology Provider**. (Chapter 5)

Small Business – a broad (but largely ambiguous) frequently misused term that describes a business organization with minimal employees and annual revenue. (All chapters)

Soft Cost – any expense incurred in using technology tools that cannot directly be accounted for and itemized as an out-of-pocket expense for product and service purchases; small businesses face many hidden computer support soft costs including needs analysis, product selection and procurement, installation, configuration, testing, customization, training, documentation, ongoing maintenance, troubleshooting and upgrading. See **Computer Support, Customization Expense, Depreciation Expense, Installation Expense, Maintenance Expense, Procurement Expense, Troubleshooting** and **Upgrade Expense**. (All chapters)

Software – programs, applications, operating systems and utilities generally developed and marketed by independent software vendors (ISVs). See **ISV (Independent Software Vendor)** and **OS (Operating System)**. (All chapters)

SOHO (Small Office/Home Office) – an acronym believed to be created by marketers and product managers to describe a way of lumping together home office and home business needs with more conventional small business needs; term generally too vague to be useful, except in reading the intentions of the company or organization proclaiming its product's or service's usefulness to the SOHO market. See **Small Business**. (All chapters)

SP/SR (Service Pack/Service Release) – jargon used by Microsoft and other ISVs for the incremental updates to software distributed in between major version upgrades; can get assistance with maintaining SP/SR levels for Microsoft Windows and Microsoft Office through Windows Update and Microsoft Office Product Updates. See **ISV (Independent Software Vendor), Maintenance Expense, Microsoft Office, Microsoft Office Product Updates, Microsoft Windows, Upgrade Expense** and **Windows Update**. (Chapter 1, Chapter 3, Chapter 4 and Chapter 5)

Spike – utility power disturbance that can cause severe damage to your hardware and data files; characterized by an extremely short burst of overvoltage; a longer duration spike is a surge. See **Hardware** and **Surge**. (Chapter 7)

Spreadsheet Software – a software application that organizes data by cells, rows, columns, ranges, worksheets and workbooks; Microsoft Excel commands the majority of U.S. and global spreadsheet market share. See **Microsoft Excel** and **Software**. (Chapter 1 and Chapter 3)

Supported Configuration – a term used by computer consultants, IT professionals and other technology vendors, such as hardware manufacturers, ISVs and ISPs, to describe the combinations of hardware, software, networking and services they can fully support. See **Computer Consultant, Hardware, ISP (Internet Service Provider), ISV (Independent Software Vendor), IT (Information Technology), Network** and **Software.** (Chapter 4)

Surge – utility power disturbance that can cause severe damage to your hardware and data files; caused by overvoltage; a very short duration surge is called a spike. See **Hardware** and **Spike.** (Chapter 7)

Surge Protector – device used to limit or divert overvoltage electrical current that can cause severe damage to your hardware and data files; also frequently referred to as a surge suppressor. See **Hardware** and **Surge.** (Chapter 7)

System Recovery Wizard (Automated) – a Microsoft Windows XP feature, dubbed ASR (Automated System Recovery) and included with the OS Backup Utility, that helps to back up and recover corrupted systems and return them to a known-good point in time. See **Microsoft Windows** and **OS (Operating System).** (Chapter 4)

System Requirements – a third-party vendor's disclosure of the minimum required *and usually* also the recommended set of hardware, software and operating system specifications a desktop PC, notebook or server must have to run a specific software application or hardware device. See **Desktop PC, Hardware, Notebook PC, OS (Operating System), Server** and **Software.** (Chapter 1)

Systems Integrator – See **Integrator.** (Chapter 1)

T

Tape Backup Drive – magnetic tape mass storage device used primarily to back up data for archiving and future disaster recovery; purpose is really for future restoration of data, so could be more aptly named a "tape restore drive"; available in many footprints and formats varying tremendously in cost, performance and capacity; popular tape backup drives used by small businesses are Travan (TR-4/TR-5) and DAT (DDS-3/DDS-4). See **DAT (Digital Audio Tape) Tape Backup Drive, DLT (Digital Linear Tape) Tape Backup Drive** and **Travan Tape Backup Drive.** (Chapter 6)

Taskbar – part of the graphical user interface (GUI) on the bottom strip of the Microsoft Windows Desktop; from left to right, displays a Start button for the Start Menu, shortcut icons for commonly used software programs, a list of all software programs currently in use, a series of icons representing software that's active or enabled whenever Microsoft Windows is booted up and a clock. See **Microsoft Windows Desktop**, **Shortcut** and **Software**. (Chapter 4 and Chapter 8)

Technology Provider – general term for any company or individual offering technology products or services and building a strong, local trusted advisor relationship with the client; can refer to an ASP, computer consultant, integrator, ISP, ISV or VAR. See **ASP (Application Service Provider)**, **Computer Consultant**, **Integrator**, **ISP (Internet Service Provider)**, **ISV (Independent Software Vendor)** and **VAR (Value Added Reseller)**. (All chapters)

Template (Microsoft Word) – a Microsoft Word file that determines the basic structural elements of a document; uses the .dot file extension by default; unless told otherwise, Microsoft Word creates all new documents (.doc files) using the Normal.dot template; small businesses can customize and create a library of Microsoft Word templates to increase employee productivity, reduce outside printing costs and enforce companywide consistency. See **Employee Productivity** and **Microsoft Word**. (Chapter 3 and Chapter 4)

Toolbar – part of a software application's user interface that graphically depicts the more commonly used commands for a software program; provides point-and-click access to the most common functions in a particular program; although not so comprehensive as pull-down menus, the concise nature of Toolbars makes them a great choice for training beginning end users; more advanced power users often navigate software through a combination of pull-down menus and Toolbars. See **Power User**, **Pull-Down Menu**, **Software** and **Training for End Users**. (Chapter 3, Chapter 4 and Chapter 5)

Training for End Users – hands-on instruction on desktop productivity software and use of shared, network resources; tends to be *much* less technical and more business-needs-oriented than training for the internal guru; training usually received from several informal approaches, with heavy emphasis on impromptu sessions with the company's internal guru or a professional computer consultant. See **Computer Consultant**, **Internal Guru**, **Network**, **Software** and **Training for the Internal Guru**. (All chapters)

Training for the Internal Guru – hands-on instruction on hardware, software, networks and telecommunications services, with particular emphasis on best practices required to maintain maximum system up-time in a small business networked environment; training usually given only to one to three employees in a small business who are en-trusted with the responsibilities of part-time internal systems administrator; training usually received from many informal ap-proaches, such as books like this and impromptu shadowing sessions with a professional computer consultant. See **Computer Consultant**, **Hardware**, **Internal Guru**, **Network**, **Small Business** and **Soft-ware**. (All chapters)

Travan Tape Backup Drive – mass storage device that uses media based on an extension of the legacy QIC (Quarter-Inch Cartridge) standard; current implementation of Travan-based tape backup drives based on the TR-5 standard, with a 10GB native/20GB compressed storage capacity; previous standards include TR-4 for 4GB native/8GB compressed storage capacity and TR-3 for 1.6GB native/3.2GB com-pressed storage capacity; offers reliable backup with a relatively low hardware purchase price, but with high-cost media and somewhat me-diocre throughput relative to DAT tape backup drives. See **DAT (Digital Audio Tape) Tape Backup Drive** and **Tape Backup Drive**. (Chapter 6)

Troubleshooting – methodical process of exploring potential PC sup-port solutions by testing one variable at a time and ruling out scenarios by process of elimination. See **Computer Support**. (All chapters)

U

UNIX – an enterprise-class operating system originally developed dec-ades ago by AT&T; as its popularity has grown, UNIX evolved into several incarnations of the OS supported by a multitude of companies and organizations, including AT&T, Hewlett Packard, IBM, Silicon Graphics and Sun Microsystems; during the 1990s an alternative Open Source version of UNIX called Linux was developed and modified by hundreds of organizations and universities around the World. See **Linux** and **OS (Operating System)**. (Chapter 4)

Upgrade Expense – computer support cost associated with transitioning from a particular hardware, software or networking product to another comparable product with presumably enhanced or more robust functionality; a combination of out-of-pocket and more subtle, harder-to-measure soft costs. See **Computer Support**, **Hardware**, **Network**, **Soft Cost** and **Software**. (See Chapter 1, Chapter 2, Chapter 3, Chapter 4, Chapter 5 and Chapter 8)

UPS (Uninterruptible Power Supply) – broad category of power protection products designed to prevent tremendously expensive damage to data during utility power fluctuations; protects against common utility power problems including sags, brownouts, blackouts, spikes and surges; also known as a battery backup unit; grouped into three UPS product levels with increasing cost, complexity, feature sets and reliability; least expensive UPS, a standby unit, and is used by the majority of small businesses; other more robust, enterprise-oriented UPS products are line interactive and online models. See **Battery Backup Unit**, **Blackout**, **Brownout**, **Sag**, **Small Business**, **Spike** and **Surge**. (Chapter 7)

USB (Universal Serial Bus) Port – hardware communications interface usually built into a computer system's motherboard, used to connect peripherals to computer systems; eventually could replace parallel and serial interfaces in PCs; originally used primarily with digital cameras and scanners, but its rapidly growing popularity proliferated into most peripheral offerings including external modems, printers and UPS units; offers far superior performance throughput and easier configuration than both parallel and serial port-based peripherals; daisy-chaining and USB hubs allow you easily to extend the number of available USB ports in a given system; supported in most 32-bit versions of Microsoft Windows except Microsoft Windows NT 4 and early versions of Microsoft Windows 95. See **Hardware**, **Microsoft Windows**, **Modem**, **Motherboard**, **Parallel Port**, **Peripheral Device**, **Serial Port** and **UPS (Uninterruptible Power Supply)**. (Chapter 2 and Chapter 7)

V

V.90 Modem Standard – a high-speed, analog modem communications standard that derived from the combination of the previous x2 and K56flex standards; although intended to support a theoretical maximum of 56Kbps throughput, it rarely does, due to FCC regulations (in the USA), the need for a digital connection to the telephone company central office (CO) on the receiving side and the limitation of supporting the 56Kbps theoretical maximum speed for downloads only; just like the earlier V.34b standard, limited to 34Kbps speed for uploads; throughput also dramatically impacted by distance to CO and condition of copper or fiber cabling between your office and CO. See **Modem**. (Chapter 2)

V.92 Modem Standard – an enhancement to the V.90 modem standard; has yet to be widely adopted by most ISPs; should offer faster upload speed, "on hold" support for Internet call waiting and quicker call setup and handshake negotiations. See **ISP (Internet Service Provider)**, **Modem** and **V.90 Modem Standard**. (Chapter 2)

Value Added Reseller (VAR) – broad term for computer reseller or integrator; historically only sold computer-related products when value-added services could be bundled into an overall solution sale. See **Integrator**. (Chapter 1)

Video Display Adapter – also known as a video graphics accelerator; a printed circuit board or chipset integrated into a computer's motherboard that allows a video monitor to communicate with PC hardware and the OS. See **Chipset**, **Hardware**, **Monitor**, **Motherboard** and **OS (Operating System)**. (Chapter 1 and Chapter 4)

Video Resolution – a description of the amount of pixels, or an approximation of dots, that can be displayed on a video monitor through a combination of the OS video device driver, video display adapter and video monitor; common resolutions used by small businesses include 800-by-600 pixels, 1,024-by-768 pixels and 1,280-by-1,024 pixels. See **Device Driver**, **Monitor**, **OS (Operating System)** and **Video Display Adapter**. (Chapter 1)

Virtual Private Network (VPN) – a way of inexpensively and rapidly creating WAN (wide area network) connections by using the public Internet backbone and secure, encrypted tunneling technology; as an alternative to expensive point-to-point leased lines from telecommunications providers, VPNs can save small businesses significant amounts of money when it comes to establishing persistent, full-time connections among branch offices, telecommuters and the main office network. See **Network** and **WAN (Wide Area Network)**. (Chapter 4 and Chapter 6)

Virus – any kind of malicious software code that can be delivered through a variety of mechanisms including conventional software media, Internet downloads, e-mail file attachments, file macros, scripting, ActiveX or Java applets, and instant-messaging software. See **E-mail** and **Software**. (Chapter 8)

W

WAN (Wide Area Network) – geographically dispersed network connecting two or more locations and generally two or more LANs (local area networks). See **LAN (Local Area Network)** and **Network**. (Chapter 5 and Chapter 6)

Web Browser Software – software used primarily to view Web sites on the Internet; also can be tapped as the universal front-end or file viewer for Intranets and extranets; most small businesses use either the Microsoft Internet Explorer (IE) or Netscape Navigator Web browser. See **Microsoft Internet Explorer** and **Software**. (Chapter 1, Chapter 3, Chapter 4, Chapter 5 and Chapter 8)

White-Box PC – also known as a PC clone; a desktop PC or server, and even sometimes a notebook PC, that's assembled by a technology provider on a small scale from a combination of generic and brand-name hardware components; a substantial percentage of small businesses in the USA and worldwide purchase "white-box" PCs as an alternative to brand-name PC products from the major PC manufacturers. See **Desktop PC**, **Hardware**, **Notebook PC**, **Server**, **Small Business** and **Technology Provider**. (Chapter 1 and Chapter 4)

Windows Explorer – also known as Exploring Windows and Windows NT Explorer in other versions of Microsoft Windows operating systems; key OS software utility for managing and viewing a hierarchy of local and networked volumes, folders, subfolders, files and other OS objects. See **Microsoft Windows**, **Network**, **OS (Operating System)** and **Software**. (Chapter 3, Chapter 4, Chapter 6 and Chapter 8)

Windows File Protection – prevents a software vendor's files from inadvertently overwriting crucial Microsoft Windows OS system files; also referred to as System File Protection under different OS contexts. See **Microsoft Windows**, **OS (Operating System)** and **Software**. (Chapter 4)

Windows Update – a free Web-based tool, similar to Microsoft Office Product Updates; automatically inventories your Microsoft Windows and Microsoft Internet Explorer installations and makes recommendations for updates to help you stay up to date with the latest Microsoft Windows and Microsoft Internet Explorer critical updates, hot fixes and service packs; packages these updates together into a single download and assists with the download and installation. See **Microsoft Internet Explorer**, **Microsoft Office Product Updates** and **Microsoft Windows**. (Chapter 5)

Word Processing Software – a software application that allows you to create, edit, view, print and store documents; Microsoft Word commands the majority of U.S. and global word processing software market share; as word processing software has evolved, many of its functions have spilled over into the realm of Web page creation and desktop publishing software. See **Microsoft Word** and **Software** (Chapter 1 and Chapter 3)

Resource Directory
PC Hardware and Peripherals

- **ACPI Power Management** -- www.acpi.info (Chapter 4)

- **APC (American Power Conversion)** -- www.apcc.com (Chapter 1 and Chapter 7)

- **CNET Shopper** -- www.shopper.com (Chapter 1)

- **Compaq Computer** -- www.compaq.com (Chapter 1 and Chapter 5)

- **Crucial Technology** -- www.crucial.com (Chapter 2)

- **Dell Asset Recovery Services** -- www.dellfinancialservices.com/solutions/asset_recovery.asp (Chapter 1)

- **Dell Computer** -- www.dell.com (Chapter 1 and Chapter 5)

- **Digi** -- www.digi.com (Chapter 2)

- **eBay** -- www.ebay.com (Chapter 1)

- **EIA Environment: Consumer Education Initiative (CEI)** -- www.eiae.org (Chapter 1)

- **Gateway** -- www.gateway.com (Chapter 1 and Chapter 5)

- **Gateway.com: Recycle/Donate Your Old PC** -- www.gateway.com/home/programs/tradein_recycle.shtml (Chapter 1)

- **Hewlett Packard** -- www.hp.com (Chapter 1, Chapter 2, Chapter 5 and Chapter 6)

- **HP Environment: Return and Recycling** -- www.hp.com/hpinfo/community/environment/recycle.htm (Chapter 1)

- **IBM** -- www.ibm.com (Chapter 1 and Chapter 5)

- **IBM PC Recycling** -- www.ibm.com/environment/ (Chapter 1)

- **IBM PC Recycling Service** -- www.ibm.com/ibm/environment/products/pcrservice.phtml (Chapter 1)

- **International Association of Electronics Recyclers** -- www.iaer.org (Chapter 1)

- **Kingston Technology** -- www.kingston.com (Chapter 2)

- **Microsoft OnNow and Power Management** -- www.microsoft.com/hwdev/onnow/ (Chapter 4)

- **Microsoft Windows Hardware Compatibility List (HCL)** -- www.microsoft.com/hcl/ (Chapter 2)

- **National Safety Council (U.S.) EPR2 Project Electronic Equipment Recyclers** -- www.nsc.org/ehc/epr2/cntctlst.htm (Chapter 1)

- **Palm** -- www.palm.com (Chapter 1)

- **SIIG** -- www.siig.com (Chapter 2)

- **TechBargains** -- www.techbargains.com (Chapter 1)

- **Xircom (Intel)** --- www.xircom.com (Chapter 2)

Software Applications and Operating Systems

- **ACPI Power Management** -- www.acpi.info (Chapter 4)

- **Adobe Downloads** -- www.adobe.com/support/downloads/ (Chapter 5)

- **Apple Mac OS X** -- www.apple.com/macosx/ (Chapter 4)

- **CNET Downloads** -- download.cnet.com (Chapter 5)

- **Computer Associates** -- www.ca.com (Chapter 6 and Chapter 8)

- **Corel** -- www.corel.com (Chapter 3)

- **Linux related Web sites (Yahoo! directory)** -- dir.yahoo.com/Computers_and_Internet/Software/O perating_Systems/UNIX/Linux/ (Chapter 4)

- **Lotus** -- www.lotus.com (Chapter 3)

- **Microsoft** -- www.microsoft.com (Chapter 1)

- **Microsoft Licensing (Open License)** -- www.microsoft.com/licensing/ (Chapter 5)

- **Microsoft Office** -- www.microsoft.com/office/ (Chapter 3 and Chapter 5)

- **Microsoft Office Download Center** -- office.microsoft.com/Downloads/ (Chapter 5)

- **Microsoft Office Product Updates** -- office.microsoft.com/ProductUpdates/ (Chapter 3 and Chapter 5)

- **Microsoft OnNow and Power Management** -- www.microsoft.com/hwdev/onnow/ (Chapter 4)

- **Microsoft TechNet Flash** -- www.microsoft.com/technet/ (Chapter 5)

- **Microsoft Windows 95** -- www.microsoft.com/windows95/ (Chapter 4)

- **Microsoft Windows 98** -- www.microsoft.com/windows98/ (Chapter 4)

- **Microsoft Windows 2000** -- www.microsoft.com/windows2000/ (Chapter 4)

- **Microsoft Windows Hardware Compatibility List (HCL)** -- www.microsoft.com/hcl/ (Chapter 2)

- **Microsoft Windows Me** -- www.microsoft.com/windowsme/ (Chapter 4)

- **Microsoft Windows NT Workstation 4.0** -- www.microsoft.com/ntworkstation/ (Chapter 4)

- **Microsoft Windows Update** -- windowsupdate.microsoft.com (Chapter 5)

- **Microsoft Windows XP** -- www.microsoft.com/windowsxp/ (Chapter 4)

- **Sun Microsystems** -- www.sun.com (Chapter 3)

- **Symantec Downloads** -- www.symantec.com/downloads/ (Chapter 5)

- **ZDNet Downloads** -- www.zdnet.com/downloads/ (Chapter 5)

Data Protection

- **APC (American Power Conversion)** -- www.apcc.com (Chapter 1 and Chapter 7)

- **APC UPS Selector** -- www.apcc.com/template/size/apc/ (Chapter 7)

- **Computer Associates** -- www.ca.com (Chapter 6 and Chapter 8)

- **Computer Associates Virus Information Center and Virus Encyclopedia** -- www3.ca.com/virus/ (Chapter 8)

- **Hewlett Packard** -- www.hp.com (Chapter 1, Chapter 2, Chapter 5 and Chapter 6)

- **Network Associates** -- www.nai.com (Chapter 8)

- **Network Associates McAfee VirusScan and NetShield products** -- www.mcafeeb2b.com/products/ (Chapter 8)

- **Network Associates Virus Information Library** -- vil.nai.com/vil/ (Chapter 8)

- **Seagate Technology** -- www.seagate.com (Chapter 6)

- **Security Administrator** -- www.secadministrator.com (Chapter 8)

- **Symantec Norton AntiVirus products** -- www.symantec.com/nav/ (Chapter 8)

- **Symantec Security Response** -- www.symantec.com/avcenter/ (Chapter 8)

- **Tripp Lite** -- www.tripplite.com (Chapter 7)

- **TruSecure** -- www.trusecure.com (Chapter 8)

- **VERITAS** -- www.veritas.com (Chapter 6)

General

- *CRN* (formerly *Computer Reseller News*) -- www.crn.com (Chapter 1)

- **Gartner Dataquest** -- www.gartner.com (Chapter 1 and Chapter 5)

- **IDC** -- www.idc.com (Chapter 6)

- **Joshua Feinberg's Small Biz Tech Talk** -- www.smallbiztechtalk.com (All chapters)

- **Microsoft Worldwide Sites** -- www.microsoft.com/worldwide/ (Chapter 5)

- *PC Magazine* -- www.pcmag.com (Chapter 1)

Companion CD-ROM

Are you ready to take your cost-savings to the next level, but you're at a loss for the *right* questions to ask? Check out the Companion CD-ROM for *What Your Computer Consultant Doesn't Want You to Know* -- with over 550 Action Items to get you started saving money right now.

The Action Items are presented in a variety of convenient file formats including Adobe Acrobat .pdf, HTML, Microsoft Word .doc and Microsoft Excel .xls. In addition, the Action Items are loaded up in a Microsoft Outlook Personal Folders File (.pst) -- ready for you to import into your Microsoft Outlook Tasks. The Companion CD-ROM also includes an electronic Resource Directory, recapping the book's suggested Web sites, that's all set for you to import into your Microsoft Internet Explorer Favorites list. Use the handy Action Item format to copy, paste and delegate -- while you tailor the money-saving program to your company's unique needs.

For more information on the Companion CD-ROM, see page 285.

Or visit www.smallbiztechtalk.com/tools/ to download sample Action Items or order the Companion CD-ROM.

Table of Tips

Index

About the Author

Joshua Feinberg is an internationally recognized small business technology expert, speaker, trainer, coach, columnist and author. He has been featured in *Business 2.0, CRN Computer Reseller News, Entrepreneurs! Tour of America Syndicated Radio Show, Network World, Purple Squirrel, South Florida Sun-Sentinel* and *Windows NT Magazine.*

Joshua's first book, *Building Profitable Solutions with Microsoft BackOffice Small Business Server 4.5* (Microsoft Press, 1999), shows computer consultants how to build a lucrative services business around the Microsoft Small Business Server (SBS) platform.

He began his career in the PC industry in 1989 and since has written more than 110 published articles for print and online media including *Selling Windows NT Solutions Magazine, Windows NT Magazine* and *Microsoft Certified Professional Magazine.*

Joshua is also the creator of and a two-year veteran columnist for *Microsoft Corporation's Direct Access* "VAPVoice: Notes From the Field," a series of 40 columns that have been syndicated, localized and translated into more than a dozen languages worldwide.

Joshua has a B.A. in Economics from Rutgers College, attended the Stern Graduate School of Business at New York University, and lives with his wife and publisher Jennifer just south of sunny West Palm Beach, Florida.

Joshua Feinberg
Small Biz Tech Talk, West Palm Beach, Florida, USA
www.smallbiztechtalk.com
letters@smallbiztechtalk.com
Phone
    Toll-Free Within the U.S. 866-TECH-EXPERT [866-832-4397]
    Within FL & Outside the U.S. +1-561-642-4220
Fax +1-561-642-7718

What Your Computer Consultant Doesn't Want You to Know

The Secrets of World Class IT on a Small Business Budget

◀ Available as a full-day, half-day or keynote presentation
◀ Fully customizable to your organization's or company's unique needs

Computer consultants offer small businesses an excellent way to tap into experienced information technology (IT) talent, without the overhead of a full-time IT manager on payroll. However, many small businesses call on their computer consultant too quickly, too often, when they could just as readily and easily handle many basic, routine computer support problems on their own.

Outsource less and save more by in-sourcing PC support tasks. Learn how to save money on computer support and related tech expenses with dozens of little-known tactics of high-priced tech consultants.

What are you waiting for?
Take control of your technology now!

Topics include
- The value of an internal guru
- How to decide which tasks to continue outsourcing
- Three inexpensive hardware devices that can prevent panic
- How to keep your software up to date -- for free
- Ways to avoid industry-specific software rip-offs
- How to lessen the risk of renting online software
- What Microsoft doesn't want you to know about buying software
- How to improve the reliability of your computer systems
- Data backup strategies that can save your company
- How to get the best deals on desktop PC and notebook purchases
- Protecting your business from the dangers of flaky utility power
- Simple virus prevention tips

To inquire about Joshua's speaking packages and availability, visit
www.smallbiztechtalk.com/workshops/

Small Biz Tech Talk® Teleclasses
We bring the learning to you!

The ultimate convenience for busy professionals

Small Business Owners/Managers, Trusted Advisors and Technology Consultants

◀ Participate from the comfort of your office, home office or virtually anywhere

◀ Optimized for the ***internal guru***, the part-time de facto computer person

Highly-targeted training on small business computer support topics

◀ Just select the 50 minute classes that are most relevant to your unique needs *and* fit in with your schedule

◀ No need to commit to a full-day off-site class

Extremely cost-effective

◀ Save Time -- No need to leave the office or sit in traffic

◀ Save Money -- No gas, tolls or parking

◀ Save a Fortune, compared to traditional classroom instruction, full-day workshops and one-on-one coaching

Value-Added

◀ Class sizes limited so time's available for Q&A and participation

◀ Classes enhanced with related online handouts, which you can download either before or during the teleclass session

What's the best way to keep in the loop on upcoming teleclasses?

◀ Subscribe to the free bi-weekly Tips newsletter at www.smallbiztechtalk.com

◀ Visit **www.smallbiztechtalk.com/teleclasses/**

Would you like a convenient way to keep up with new tips and techniques from Small Biz Tech Talk?

Subscribe to the free bi-weekly Tips newsletter at www.smallbiztechtalk.com

Take Control of Your Technology Now!

Small Biz Tech Talk®
www.smallbiztechtalk.com

10 Cool Keyboard Shortcuts for Small Biz Tech Talk Groupies

Keyboard Shortcut	Function	Software Applications
Ctrl + Enter	Appends "www." and ".com" to a Web site URL	Microsoft Internet Explorer
Ctrl + ; Ctrl + :	Enters today's date and the current time	Microsoft Excel
Ctrl + A	Select All	Microsoft Windows and Microsoft Office
Ctrl + C Ctrl + V	Copy and Paste	Microsoft Windows and Microsoft Office
Ctrl + N	Opens a new Window or new file	Microsoft Internet Explorer, Microsoft Word, Microsoft Excel
Ctrl + X Ctrl + V	Cut and Paste	Microsoft Windows and Microsoft Office
F2	Rename, Edit	Microsoft Windows and Microsoft Excel
F5	Refresh and Send/Receive	Microsoft Internet Explorer and Microsoft Outlook
Windows key + D	Minimizes all open Windows to display Windows Desktop	Microsoft Windows (multiple versions)
Windows key + E	Launches Windows Explorer	Windows Explorer

What Your Computer Consultant Doesn't Want You to Know

101 Money-Saving Secrets of Expensive Techies

Take Control of Your Technology with the *Ultimate* Small Business Do-It-Yourself Guide

No small business manager, internal guru or trusted advisor should contract for computer consulting until after reading this book!

Don't let another week pass in which your consultant is building a hefty invoice and withholding key training to create job security at your expense.

What are you waiting for?

Take control of your technology now!

288 pages, ISBN 0-9714153-8-2
Glossary, Resource Directory, Index
$19.99 USA

By Joshua Feinberg

Creator of Microsoft Corporation's Direct Access *Notes from the Field*

Author of *Building Profitable Solutions with Microsoft BackOffice Small Business Server*

As Seen in *Business 2.0, CRN, NetworkWorld, Selling Windows NT Solutions, South Florida Sun-Sentinel* and *Windows NT Magazine*

Foreword by Jeff Zbar

U.S. SBA 2001 Small Business Journalist of the Year

www.smallbiztechtalk.com

8 More Cool Web Sites for Small Biz Tech Talk Groupies

- **BusinessWeek Technology** --
  www.businessweek.com/technology/

- **Broadband Reports/DSL Reports** --
  www.dslreports.com

- **Gibson Research** -- www.grc.com

- **Inc. Information Technology** --
  www.inc.com/information_technology/

- **Register.com** -- www.register.com

- **The Wall Street Journal Personal Technology**
  -- ptech.wsj.com

- **Webopedia** -- www.webopedia.com

- **Windows & .NET Magazine Network** --
  www.winnetmag.com

Add don't forget to bookmark
Small Biz Tech Talk -- www.smallbiztechtalk.com

Small Biz Tech Talk®

What Your Computer Consultant
Doesn't Want You to Know

Toll Free (866) 832-4397
[866 TECH-EXPERT]

+1 (561) 642-4220

customersvc@smallbiztechtalk.com

www.smallbiztechtalk.com

PO Box 541958, Greenacres, FL, USA 33467
Fax +1 (561) 642-7718

What are you waiting for?
Take Control of Your Technology Now!

Small Biz Tech Talk® Press Order Form

What Your Computer Consultant Doesn't Want You To Know

Name _____ Company _____

Address _____

City _____ State/Province _____ Zip/Postal _____ Country _____

Telephone _____ E-mail Address _____

Quantity of Books *   _____ @ $19.99 USA

Quantity of Companion CD-ROMs *   _____ @ $39.99 USA

Quantity of Audio Courses *   _____ @ $149.00 USA

                   Subtotal $_____

                   Shipping ** $_____

                   Sales Tax (FL only: 6%) $ _____

Method of Payment: **Total $ _____**

__ Enclosed is my check/money order payable to Small Biz Tech Talk (U.S. funds)
__ Please charge the above to my credit card (Visa, MasterCard, Amex, Discover):

Card Number _____ Expiration ____/____

Signature _____ Date ____/____/____

Cardholder Name _____

Cardholder Billing Address _____

* **Volume Discount** available on orders of 10 or more. Call or e-mail for details.
** **Shipping**   *Within the U.S.* $6 for 1st product ($2 for each additional)
                       Canada $7 for 1st product ($3 for each additional)
                       International $9 for 1st product ($5 for each additional)

90 Day Money Back Guarantee

If you are not 100 percent convinced and satisfied that Joshua Feinberg's knowledge and experience can help you, simply return the products in resalable condition along with your sales receipt for a complete, no hassle refund.

To order, contact Small Biz Tech Talk Press

Toll Free (866) 832-4397 [866 TECH-EXPERT] *or* +1 (561) 642-4220
PO Box 541958, Greenacres, FL, USA 33467   Fax +1 (561) 642-7718
customersvc@smallbiztechtalk.com   www.smallbiztechtalk.com